FAT GAY VEGAN

*Dedicated to anyone who wants
to do better and be kinder*

FAT GAY VEGAN

EAT, DRINK AND LIVE LIKE YOU GIVE A SH!T

SEAN O'CALLAGHAN

NOURISH

EAT WELL, LIVE WELL

This edition published in the UK and USA 2018 by
Watkins, an imprint of Watkins Media Limited
19 Cecil Court
London WC2N 4EZ

enquiries@watkinspublishing.com

1 3 5 7 9 10 8 6 4 2

Typeset by seagulls.net

Printed and bound in the United Kingdom

A CIP record for this book is available from the British Library

ISBN: 978-1-84899-351-8

www.nourishbooks.com

CONTENTS

iNTRODUCTiON

> Deep down we all want to do the right thing, even though sometimes we get thrown off track by forces seemingly bigger than us.

'I follow your Instagram. I love your name!'

'Hey. Are you that big gay vegan?'

'Excuse me. Do you write a blog about being fat and gay?'

'Are you … no, I don't want to say it. I don't want to hurt your feelings!'

If this is the first time you are encountering me as Fat Gay Vegan you are probably intrigued, or at the very least tickled slightly, by the name. Of all the things I have done during the decades spent marauding around on this fragile planet, being FGV is far and away the one that is set to have the most impact, especially when I consider the sheer number of people it has allowed me to connect with around the globe. I will get on to what it is exactly I do, but before I get to singing my own praises and lecturing you on how to be a decent vegan, I really should give the unfamiliar amongst you an insight into the origins of Fat Gay Vegan.

During a strange time in history before the *Twilight* trilogy but after the Pete Wentz nude photos leak, I was a prolific blogger on a social media platform where selfies-before-they-were-called-selfies were currency and eyeliner was plentiful and thick. Yes kids, I was a MySpace blogger. If you dodged the Fall Out Boy fans and the painfully-slow-to-load custom backgrounds and found yourself on my page, you would have been given a glimpse into what made me tick. Long story short is that I ticked thanks to travel, vegan food, the fight for animal rights, a love of pop music and gay stuff like Pride marches and the rise of Lady Gaga.

I spent a year or two writing vegan restaurant reviews from around Australia and the USA that weren't as witty as I would have like to have believed, and then MySpace experienced an undignified fall from grace that left vegan bloggers and emo kids in the wilderness. We had a lot of feelings about things and the world needed to know about them.

Even though veganism first entered my life in 1999, it was in 2010, after arriving in the UK for what has turned into a more than seven-year residency, that I was ready to make a bigger commitment to the activist side of myself. I decided to contribute to building the vegan scene in London and I thought a blog would be a fine way of bringing people together, both online and eventually in real life at social events.

I decided to start a blog because I enjoyed the platform as a way of expressing myself, and I had come to realise that getting feedback from readers was a big motivation for me. As such, to get people to come back regularly and take notice of what I had to say, I needed to make my blog a little bit more focussed. My musings over on MySpace swung wildly from flippant critiques of the latest Britney Spears melodrama to tasty vegan taquitos I devoured during a vacation to Berkeley. The blog needed more of an identity so, based on my burgeoning interest in animal rights, I settled on becoming a vegan blogger.

A blog name will make you or break you. There are so many almost-identical names out there in the wild west of the World Wide Web and I didn't want to be just another 'plant-based' somebody or 'it's just me being kooky' narcissist. There were already enough glowing, vital and vibrant vegan bloggers flooding the scene when I decided to stick my chubby hand up in the air.

Fat Gay Vegan as a name was a few years in the making. The idea of using words that have often been used to pigeonhole me or hurt me started back during a university presentation. I was tasked with performing a representation of my personality so, in a completely cloying exhibition of self-indulgence, I stood under a single spotlight wearing giant swing tags hanging around my neck. Please don't laugh. Each tag had a different word written on it, words that I felt were weighing me down in life. Gay. Faggot. Fat. Sissy. Vegan. You get the idea. One by one, I lifted the tags from around my neck and dropped them to the floor as a symbolic gesture of freeing myself from hurtful labels. I'm actually cringing as I type this.

Skip forward a few years and I found myself joking around during a conversation with a friend about how people viewed me as somehow deficient because I was fat, gay and vegan. Those labels were often used to ridicule me in various situations and I was keen to find a way to reclaim and reappropriate them. When the idea of a blog started to develop, my online personality Fat Gay Vegan started to take on a life of its own as the fun-loving, potato-obsessed good time chubby guy with a heart of gold. I've lost track of the number of times someone has told me they started following me on social media because of the name alone.

There are a lot of negative social connotations surrounding being a fat person and believe me when I say I've experienced setbacks and discrimination as a gay person throughout my life. The vegan part of me gets fed up as well with people I know and don't know making judgements and jokes about my compassion as though it's the funniest thing they have encountered. Taking these three words that are sometimes used to belittle me and turning them into a positive badge of honour has been wonderful.

I've created an inclusive online community that has spilled over into real-life events I host, meaning people have come to associate the name Fat Gay Vegan with positivity and compassion. The FGV platform is known for helping people go and stay vegan in order to improve outcomes for animals. I've learned to love hearing the words Fat Gay Vegan come out of stranger's mouths now as they are mostly spoken by happy people looking to share goodwill with me. Words that were once used to make me feel bad or different have become a celebration for me and it feels incredible to have that connected with caring for animals.

There is also something to be said for getting people to say the words out loud in public. Each time my blog name is mentioned in a crowd, it feels like a tiny political act of defiance and irreverence. I've stopped letting people use those words to hurt me and hearing them spoken back to me in a positive manner helps to reinforce that victory.

That's me out of the way. I think I've clearly established myself as Fat Gay Vegan. If you have any questions, I'm happy to meet you over a cold pint (you are paying, right?) to sort out any confusion. I've got a book to introduce to you.

So you know by now that I'm not a celebrity chef and I'm not a superstar nutritionist. What can I bring to a book about veganism – other than overeating, all the ways potato can be prepared and my love of beer, pop music and deep-fried comfort food?

I think that I do hold a unique view of veganism from which I hope that others will be able to draw some inspiration. I have lived a vegan lifestyle for almost two decades; I've experienced being vegan in various countries, and I've seen this movement shift from the fringes to mainstream newspaper articles, celebrity vegans and giant vegan shows welcoming ten thousand people. You can't go through life interacting with the number of vegan people that I do without learning a thing or two of value to bring to the conversation.

I want to help people and one of my biggest desires is for people to feel cherished and celebrated for their choice to live a vegan life. My dedication to being compassionate towards animals is inseparable from my commitment to caring for oppressed people and challenging discrimination in all forms.

So that's the basis of this book. I want to talk with you about doing the best you can for animals while never forgetting that our responsibilities are much broader than just veganism. I believe that a life spent caring for non-human animals but ignoring or contributing unchecked to the oppression of humans is not a truly compassionate life. There is no reason why we can't explore and expand all aspects of our empathetic selves as we learn and grow into a vegan life.

This all-encompassing approach to a compassionate life is my own and I fully accept it might not be exactly what everyone wants to hear, but I'd be shocked if someone could honestly say there isn't something in this book that resonates with them. I think kindness is a universal goal, even if sometimes we get there on different paths and routes. If you want the best for people, animals and the planet then I think we will get along just fine together during your time with this book.

Deep down, we all want to do the right thing, even though sometimes we get thrown off track by forces that seem bigger than us. We try to buy sweatshop-free clothing, we try to speak up against bigotry, and we think kind thoughts about people we know and don't know. I hope this book can be a little collection of reminders on how to stay on the ethical straight and narrow while we work to improve outcomes for animals. I try my best to be an inclusive person and not contribute to the oppression of other humans, but I still need my safety nets and reminders. I often call on friends to remind me of best practice when it comes to being caring, I watch documentaries and I read articles and books about resisting oppression. Whether you are a long-time vegan or someone on the cusp of starting your vegan journey, maybe this book can become a small tool in your toolbox of tricks to do better.

This book is an exploration of what living a vegan lifestyle actually translates to in the real world, from shopping for food to travelling the world. It's also an exploration of what veganism means to me, what it means to a few of my friends, and how we made the connection between our actions and the treatment of animals. I offer advice on being a compassionate consumer, but I also explore how you might manage your interpersonal relationships with non-vegans and find ways to be respectful and inclusive while remaining steadfastly vegan.

You are going to find useful tips on how to stay a happy, committed and effective vegan. But it isn't all FGV telling you what to do. I can tell you about being a fat gay vegan, but I'm not equipped or entitled to tell you about experiences that I don't live through. There are stories about the experiences of certain vegans that I felt were crucial to this book and really helpful for the wider conversation, so I've reached out to friends, colleagues and people I admire in order to give a broader range of voices to these pages. Parts of the book might feel like I'm rolling out a cavalcade of minority superstars to tick a progressive checklist, but the only other option was a white man telling you why you shouldn't be sexist, racist, ableist and transphobic. That's not how it works, kids.

Every voice included in this book has been asked to participate in order to help us build an understanding of how we can do better to fight oppression. A lot of the people I call on are my friends and not only do I love them, I also happen to think they are superbly smart and switched on. It's an honour to have them in these pages and I'm certain you will appreciate their contributions.

However, to give you a break from my righteous posturing I have included some of my favourite meal ideas as end of chapter rewards. I love the idea of some of you taking a break from the book to slip into the kitchen for mashed potato taquitos and cheesy chipotle popcorn.

This book is a glimpse into what makes me tick. I walked away from a career as a schoolteacher because I felt that I had something important to say as a vegan who also cares about humans. The events I run are designed to make people happier vegans and the blog I write daily is designed to support independent vegan business. It is a struggle to make money, pay my bills and remain stress-free but I do it because I believe it is making a difference.

But what about the animals? You came here because you care about the animals, right? This book isn't a collection or rundown of the worst things humans can do to animals. Yes, I refer to the mistreatment and suffering to which animals are subjected but I know you are not stupid or ill informed. I'm not keen on insulting your intelligence by telling you on every page that animals have feelings and that humans cut their throats. You know this already. You're holding this book because you are already on a journey of expanding your compassion for animals. I'm here to keep you company, pat you on the back, and remind you that you can do it. Everything in this book is to help improve outcomes for animals, even if at times it doesn't feel like the intention. You can't do the right thing for animals to the best of your ability if you're not working on being aware of all forms of oppression.

My one true desire for this book is for people to read with an open mind and heart. Even if you're not yet a vegan, and don't think you're going to be one soon, I want you to know that this book has been written for you as much as it has been for long-term vegans. If there is something you come across that doesn't sit happily with you straight away, it's OK to reflect and come back to it at a later date. Hey, it's even OK to disagree with me. The most I can ask of you is that you listen to what I have to say. Thank you for your time and thank you for joining me on this journey of ethical veganism. I'm already loving your company!

CHAPTER ONE
WHY VEGAN?

It takes knowing the facts, knowing your part and feeling it is the right thing to do in your heart.

As strange as it might sound, I'm not going to start this chapter by immediately telling you why I am a vegan. That would be too obvious, right?

Don't fret. I'll get to the sanctimonious lecturing in good time! My vegan journey is poured onto these pages like a bucket of plant-based honey alternative. You won't be able to scrub my sticky story of compassionate transformation from your pleather pumps by the end of these pages.

I'd like to tell you a slightly older tale from personal experience to help us get acquainted. I want you to know where I came from so you understand how alike we are. This is my devious trick, you see. When a wave of realisation swamps you and you come to learn how incredibly simple and sensible choosing veganism is, you'll have me sitting up there in your head like a friendly, fat uncle whispering, 'I knew you could do it'.

The day will arrive when you proclaim, 'Hey, if that fat gay guy can do it, so can I!'

Please take my hairy hand as we step back in time to an Australia where Hugh Jackman was yet to transform into Wolverine, Paul Hogan was a national hero and the most a queer kid like me could hope for was to somehow get the hell out of my hometown.

In my early years growing up in Australia, animals were close to impossible to escape. As a young person (who was gay but not yet fat or vegan), I was confronted by the existence of animals on a daily basis in the seaside town I often reluctantly called home. They were on my plate, in my lunchbox, in the ocean, on my television and on my body in the form of clothing.

For a major part of my formative years, my mother and I lived in a budget caravan park on the Queensland coast. If this conjures up images of jellyfish, sharks and animal agriculture then you're about right. It was both an extreme yet simple experience where my biggest worry was crossing the sleepy main road in one piece in order to pick up our dinner from the fish and chip shop. I never forgot to slip in an order of battered sausages or spin Prince on the jukebox with whatever coins I could scrape together.

I can't be certain that this area of the world is where the term 'surf and turf' originated, but it most definitely did its best to claim a place in history as the steak and seafood capital. My mother would take me to pubs and cafés where servers in open footwear and pastel-splashed Hypercolor t-shirts (remember?) would hand us oversized menus highlighting multiple ways to prepare a cut of meat. If my memory serves me correctly, my go-to meal was usually a prawn cocktail. Net-caught sea creatures were crumbed and fried before being served to me in a frosted, fancy glass with tangy sauce dripping down the side.

My childhood was what polite society refers to as 'lower socioeconomic', but it's simpler to say poor when you are reflecting on not having stepped inside a permanent structure for most of your pre-pubescent years. My days were spent climbing the nearby cliffs to watch fishing trawlers dragging my inexpensive pub lunch back to the shore, all the while seagulls the size of footballs relentlessly squawked, circled and dive-bombed in the wake of the boats. If I were fortunate enough (or patient enough), I would see dolphins or whales passing between my rocky perch and the neighbouring island across the sun-drenched bay. I didn't know where these creatures were going, or from where they had travelled for that matter. All I knew was that they were getting away from the poor boy living on the beach, just the same as the passengers reclining inside the jumbo jets soaring past the eternally-hungry seagulls and into the impossibly blue sky above me.

When the sun became too hot, or the salt spray from the sea made me uncomfortable, I would clamber down from the crumbly, red cliffs and make my way back along the sandy cove littered with pine cones, polished glass fragments and intricately twisted driftwood. These daily saunters along the beach would regularly throw up unexpected but not entirely uncommon surprises.

One late summer afternoon, I saw ahead of me, along the shoreline, a group of sun-kissed children and teenagers were huddled around a shallow tide pool. I passed by the shiny sand trinkets that would normally arrest my attention, thinking that something more worthwhile must be on the beach ahead. Beach kids have nothing to do most of the time and it doesn't take much to reel them in, but this was a sizeable crowd that suggested big time excitement.

I jostled into a position that wasn't quite front row, but close enough to peer over the shoulders of some of the shorter children. Crashing and splashing in a tidal pool right there in front of my eyes was a shark. No, not a Jaws-sized monster from the depths that had come onto land in order to exact revenge on the family of a human that had aggrieved it during the mid-70s. This shark stranded in the tidal pool was a compact fish only two feet in length at most. Of course, anyone within arms' reach who had a stick or a branch thought it was the height of danger and excitement to prod and poke the trapped creature. It frantically churned the shallow pool until it was too tired to resist. It had apparently resigned itself to float there and take its prodding.

My memory isn't iron clad all these decades later. What could have been seconds or minutes passed when suddenly an adult, with the same annoyed face that all adults have when children are being troublesome, stormed over to our group. Pushing us out of the way, he picked the shark up by its tail and tossed it into the murky ocean.

Being outside in nature all day has a way of bringing you closer to life and death. One day, with my family on one of our trips to the island across the bay, we spotted a giant sea turtle burying eggs in the late-night moonlight. Then, sometime later, our group of beachcomber explorers came across another turtle. It was mammoth and dead – a giant bite taken from part of its shell and flesh. I was quick to attribute this particular mystery to the real Jaws, although a few of the older children who fancied themselves Nancy Drew types were adamant a ship propeller was the culprit.

I often wonder if it was the same turtle. Or maybe it was one of the babies that survived the tumultuous journey from the sandy nest to the choppy waves.

Fishing with my father was a life and death situation of which I do not have fond memories, mostly due to the fact that my father was an awful person in every sense of the word. Don't worry, he can't sue the publishers of this book or take offence. He died a few years ago and is now filed away with the tragic sea turtle and cut-price, net-caught prawns.

My father, with who I was forced to spend time every second weekend against my better judgement and wishes, would take me out onto a cold, dark pier so I could experience him threading live worms onto hooks that would hopefully catch fish by the mouth. I don't recall having that much of an inkling of the cruelty of fishing at the time, but I vividly remember how utterly despondent I was during these trips. The fish would flop and splash in the bucket of which I was always inexplicably left in charge, while my father would berate me for not being manly enough to join in. I was probably about five years old at the time, but these experiences gave me an understanding of the connection between treating humans and animals kindly. He might not have been the best father, but at least I took this lesson away from the situation.

I read a lot as a child and books were my luxurious escape from reality. One book that caught my attention was a sad tale of an outsider boy named Andy. Titled *I Own the Racecourse!* and written by Patricia Wrightson, the story followed the somewhat unfortunate child who was duped into believing he had bought the local horseracing track for loose change from a homeless man. Books for children were not happy affairs back in my day, that's for certain.

Inspired by my anti-hero of the depressing novel, I would sometimes leave my beachside haunts and visit the racetrack situated a few blocks from the ocean. The abandoned announcers box was the perfect outpost for me to spy on the powerful horses as they were whipped to run around the circuit as people cheered and guzzled beer in the shiny new stands made from glass and glistening steel. The horses fascinated me for unknown reasons. I was never a horse fanatic as a child but something about these horses in this location captivated me.

Horse racing in Australia was served up to us as a jingoistic pastime in which school children were expected to take an interest in order to be considered solid citizens. The Melbourne Cup is a race that apparently 'stops the nation' each November and my school was no exception. Australian schools had television sets on roll-able trolleys and the Melbourne Cup meant a set was rolled into the classroom to enable us to watch the race.

One of the more responsible students was tasked with walking between classrooms with an empty ice cream tub that had a slot cut into the lid, into which teachers would place their bets in the staff sweepstakes. It was nothing if not confusing for the young children being expected to watch animals forced to run as the adults charged with their care placed bets.

My auntie Jackie once took me to the circus and you had better believe me when I say the animals outnumbered the humans. I lost track of the number of creatures forced to jump through flaming hoops, walk on wires or drive tiny motor vehicles.

I had grown a lot taller than other children my age by the time my circus trip was foisted upon me and the donkey assigned to carry me around the ring did not look pleased with the prospect. My brown-corduroy adorned legs dragged in the dirt as the hot lights beat down and depraved-looking clowns smirked at the tall kid on the sad donkey. I'm fairly certain that was my final experience

at any form of circus, but I think more due to the
mortification and shame felt by me rather than concern for
animal welfare.

Christmas in my hometown was always brutal. First
of all, it was always sweltering hot and furthermore we
had the joy of sitting around with relatives ranging from
mildly to wildly racist. Animals featured heavily Christmas
day, from the pig-now-called-ham wrapped in a water-
soaked pillow case to keep it fresh to the family dog sitting
under the table hoping for scraps. Prawns, crabs, chickens
and turkeys who used to all be alive at some point were
scattered around the buffet in order for me and the people
I didn't like all that much to experience festive cheer.

So, animals were absolutely everywhere in my life as
a child in Australia, but I honestly didn't give them much
more thought than what I have described above. Not one
adult explained to me the difference between prawns on
the table and the dog under it. Understanding how animals
lived and died was not my concern. I was socialised into
thinking animals were available to eat, wear and prod with
sticks unquestionably.

That's what I think I have in common with a lot of you
turning these pages right this moment.

Reflect for a moment on just how much animals were
used in your young life, but how little thought was given

to the how, what, when and why. Did adults and people responsible for your emotional growth explain the process of factory farm to dining table? The shark took a chunk from the turtle just as I watched crabs being boiled alive in my kitchen at Christmas time, but they were all just 'things' in my mind. Objects. Just like the pine cones and the cliffs and the polished glass fragments at the seaside. I didn't understand that these animals were capable of fear and pain because nobody told me, and I would bet my last block of tofu they didn't tell you either.

You ate meat and so did I. We didn't think there was anything wrong with eating meat. Maybe people you love ate meat and still do? See, we are not that different. My melancholic beachside years stuffed with whimsical dreaming atop red, crumbling cliffs were just as animal-centric as your (insert geographic location and descriptors here) upbringing.

We were all socialised to expect animals to be there for us. On our tables. On our feet and backs. On our televisions, in our backyards and at our circuses. It was a way of the world that we were never expected to challenge. Popular culture actually suggested it was weird NOT to partake in the consumption of animals.

But I saw something different that made me want to choose a meat-free way of living, followed shortly after by veganism. But what was powerful enough to snap this particular human out of decades of social conditioning?

*

My late teens can be most accurately described as a wild ride. I dropped out of school on my fifteenth birthday, moved out of home, found myself in full time employment and hit the gay bar scene in the nearest big city. I thought I was a mixture of Robert Smith from The Cure and Siobhan Fahey from Bananarama. What I couldn't shoplift from a second-hand clothing store, I didn't wear.

My friends and I earned enough money working in shoe stores and supermarkets to go out dancing each and every weekend drenched in eyeliner and body spray marketed at teenage women. I struggled to keep food on my table but of course did what any well-trained human believed was correct and made sure meat was on my plate during most meals. My shopping list was atrocious and any given week it would include cheap boxes of white wine and even cheaper supermarket sausages plastic wrapped to bloodstained Styrofoam trays. I had been conditioned effectively and only went without animal protein when I couldn't afford it or had only enough cash to catch the train to the club district. I always chose a party over being well fed.

It was during these outrageous and sometimes scary years that I started to meet a type of person that had previously never crossed my path. I actually didn't know what 'vegetarian' meant the first time somebody told me that's how they identified. Of course I listened to Morrissey explain animal cruelty in confronting detail on *Meat is Murder* by The Smiths, but I honestly didn't have a framework through which to process vegetarianism. I was so very young and frankly quite emotionally stunted.

I was introduced to Vanessa and we became friendly, if not best friends. She was best friends with one of my best friends, meaning we found ourselves playing records and drinking cheap vodka together on more than a few occasions. When our group all decided that our small city was far too claustrophobic for the likes of us, we all migrated to the bright lights and plentiful temptations of Sydney.

Vanessa and I lived in a share house. She would eat vegetarian food and be made fun of for it, while I ordered fried chicken on an over-the-limit credit card on which I couldn't afford to make payments. You see, the takeaway delivery shop wouldn't run a credit check if the order was under fifty dollars. My diet was an appalling mix of grease, chicken meat, mashed potato and gravy. Looking back, I honestly can't recall how many times that meal entered my house by way of fraudulent means. I often feel bewildered with how I got away with it for so long.

In a way that I would later come to understand as a powerful form of activism and persuasion, Vanessa said very little about my dependence on dead chicken. It was almost as though her being there and being vegetarian was enough to plant a seed of thought in my mind. She didn't try to shame me. She didn't present me with horrifying tales of slaughterhouse massacres as though it was all my fault. Vanessa lived without meat and let me live as me.

But the seed was planted and sooner or later something was bound to make a connection.

A small group of us had taken a shopping trip by car to the western suburbs of Sydney on a day when the surface of the sun was seemingly touching Australia. The car interior was stifling. Vanessa or my dear-friend-still-to-this day Steven was behind the wheel, while I slumped on the back seat no doubt making moaning noises about the injustice of the heat. We were in gridlock on a motorway with the usual travel time of under an hour disappearing faster than my will to live.

Raising my head to mop my sodden brow, I glanced to the left just as a large truck rolled to a stop beside our vehicle. Piled high, with far less fresh oxygen than I was enjoying, were more chickens than I could count. The animals were crammed inside metal cages that in turn were stacked deep and wide to create some sort of Death Star semi-trailer.

My first reaction was to bemoan the unbearable stench, however my personal discomfort quickly gave way to a deep sadness. Now, you might think I was the dimmest young adult in the wider Sydney region, but this was the first time in my life I was able to make a connection between real, alive-and-scratching animals and my food choices. The over-the-limit credit card chicken dinner I had eaten countless times previously and was probably planning on eating that very night was still alive and suffering intensely beside me on a molten Sydney motorway.

I felt horrendous and guilt-ridden. There was no getting around the fact that my decision to buy fried chicken was directly linked to the demand that forced those terrified animals onto the back of that truck. I was the demand and they were the sad, suffering supply.

I can't recall if it was the next day or the next week when I watched a television news report about a truck full of cows that had overturned on a dusty outback road. Just as the chickens had, cattle now quickly became individual cows to me as I watched them stagger dazed throughout the broken bodies of their travelling companions.

I never ate meat again. It had become crystal clear to me that I had to make better choices and it was no longer satisfactory to think I was exempt from blame just because everyone else did it. Looking back, I am extremely thankful to those individual chickens and cows I saw suffering so horribly. They were the emotional catalyst I needed and decades later I still think of them and feel deep culpability.

It was shortly after my meat-free awakening that I met my partner, Josh. To illustrate how unusual it was to be vegetarian in Australia at the time, I felt the need to come out as one to him on the train as we headed to our first dinner date. The relief I felt when he informed me he too was vegetarian almost made me cry. I knew I really liked Josh and was mortified by the thought of having to sit across from a steak dinner as I attempted to woo him. Instead, we enjoyed our first romantic dinner together in a restaurant named Has Beans. Surely nothing more needs to be said on that restaurant name.

My vegetarianism never wavered and my relationship with Josh grew. For the first time in my life I left Australia. We set up home back in his native United Kingdom and the different attitude people demonstrated toward vegetarians stunned me. Even Burger King had a bean burger on the menu. A visit to my friend's family in Liverpool had them pulling meat-free sausages from the deep freezer just so I didn't miss out on the fry up they were all enjoying. Nobody laughed at me.

I could very well have travelled through life indefinitely thinking I was the height of compassion if it wasn't for one pesky little invention known as the World Wide Web.

Josh and I invested in some painfully slow dial up Internet connection and it was a revelation. The Internet was the late nineties version of that chicken truck pulling up beside me in western Sydney, but this time I was being awakened to my culpability in the suffering of egg laying birds and milk producing cows. Via rudimentary chat groups and early versions of forums, I started to be exposed to people who opted out of relying on any and all animal-derived products.

I was so reliant on milk and cheese at the time I went into shut down. Wasn't it enough to not eat the animals? Surely I was to be applauded for my commitment to animal welfare? Then I discovered that many wines are treated with animal products like egg whites, milk protein or fish products to get rid of some of the leftover solids. This sent me into a complete tailspin. There I was thinking nobody loved animals more than I, while cows were being forcibly impregnated in order for me to guzzle their milk. Cows need to be pregnant or new mothers for their bodies to produce milk and as we know, mammals don't get pregnant on their own. The discovery that dairy cows went through pregnancy repeatedly for my milk was confronting. Chickens, even those advertised as cage free, were wildly mistreated in shocking conditions for my occasional egg habit including my desire for albumen, or egg-white clarified red wine.

There must have been a few weeks of this information dripping through to me during which I still consumed dairy and sipped wine from the corner store. I needed to be slapped into a different state of understanding. I needed to truly understand the role I was playing in animal exploitation.

Enter my sister, Monique.

Monique and her partner Drew were living with us in London. They were both carnivorous without waiver and it wasn't just on one occasion I walked into the shared kitchen to discover my sister wrist deep inside a chicken carcass. The relationship I had back then with my sister was tumultuous and she would try to catch me out on any perceived flaw, real or imagined. She got a good one to ride me on with my hypocrisy surrounding animals. The day Monique sneered at me and called me a hypocrite, for saying I loved animals while refusing to give up wine from the corner shop, plays back like it was yesterday.

In a rare instance of calmness and clarity, I told my sister she was absolutely right. I could no longer drink non-vegan wine, eat dairy-containing food or buy clothing made with animal products. I went vegan that very second and have never stopped being vegan.

When people ask me for advice on how to go and stay vegan, I often retell the story of my sister pushing me into a corner. That was my defining moment and I tell people theirs will arrive. It takes knowing the facts, knowing your part and feeling it is the right thing to do in your heart. Once the pieces fall into place and you have a clear understanding of your role in reducing animal suffering, choosing vegan becomes an epiphany. It's the right thing to do and you do it. The clarity or the logic or the unavoidability of what you have come to understand puts you on a path of lifelong compassion and it's a fabulous feeling.

As a vegan blogger and event planner, I get to hear countless versions of 'the moment that made me vegan' story and I never tire of hearing them. Each one is unique and always touching. Something profound happens to make someone alter how they see their place in the world and that is a wonderful tale to share.

So I asked a few friends to walk me through their choice to live vegan. I've picked a few highlights from the chats so you can consider how important it is to have a true understanding of why veganism is important if the compassionate choice is going to stick. You'll see that my friends experienced a similar journey to mine. The decision to go vegan and stay vegan usually requires a combination of having clear information about what happens to animals and believing in your heart you can make a difference.

My partner Josh reminded me that he had been a vegetarian from age eleven when a school friend asked him why he wouldn't eat his pet dog but was comfortable eating other creatures. Yes, that old chestnut. This kickstarted a compassionate way of living for Josh that saw him never returning to his previous meat-consuming ways.

A chance encounter with a friend of a friend at age fifteen led Josh to his first brush with veganism. His group had been aimlessly hanging out in Soho trying to channel the grunge aesthetic of Kurt and Courtney when this new acquaintance (who shall remain nameless mostly due to Josh not being able to remember, but if he had to give it a good shot he says he would go with Moon) discovered that Josh was vegetarian, and launched into a lecture about his hypocrisy. Moon demanded to know why he wasn't vegan if he professed to love animals so very much.

Josh recalls this act of shaming was enough to turn him to veganism for about six months, however it didn't stick. 'I guess I didn't have a true understanding of the ethical reasons for turning down dairy or eggs, nor did I have any social or peer support,' Josh lamented to me.

This experience of being shamed into veganism only to find it doesn't stick is not uncommon amongst the vegans I know. Giving facts AND support without shaming seems to be a more effective approach when it comes to establishing long term vegans.

But back to Josh for a moment.

He remembers (like I do) the Internet playing a big part in helping his veganism stick the second time around. One of our favourite websites to visit back in the early days of the World Wide Web was a Prince (or more correctly, at the time known by a trademarked symbol and often referred to as 'the artist formerly known as Prince') portal that included, amongst other curios, a vegan recipe section. Josh recalls these recipes giving him that push to start considering taking on a plant-based diet once again. This newly piqued interest in animal-free living, combined with the ever-growing well of information available about the cruelty of the dairy and egg industries, was enough to take Josh to the point of no return as far as his veganism was concerned.

Josh reflected, 'It had never occurred to me that cheese was linked to the death and mistreatment of cows. I honestly thought cows lived blissfully in fresh fields, giving milk happily to anyone willing to pull up a wooden stool. Of course they never had to watch their offspring be dragged away into the unknown, right? I started to understand how I could lessen the demand for products and services which contributed to animal cruelty.'

I find my friend Deborah's vegan story fascinating, mostly due to the fact of how very long she lived as a vegetarian before making the change.

'I was veggie for twenty-seven years and thought I was doing a good thing for the animals, I really thought I was a good veggie,' Deborah told me. 'I never bought new leather and justified buying shoes from second hand or charity shops by telling myself I wasn't contributing to the demand.' Deborah always checked if the cheese she was being served was suitable for vegetarians, thinking she was educating people about rennet. However, she sometimes would consume these things herself because there was no alternative or because friends had made her something without realising, or occasionally because it was easier. 'A few times I ate fish and honestly I can't explain to you why because there was no need. People around me were eating it and I just joined in, justifying it to myself that fish live a wild existence and are not farmed so it couldn't be cruel.'

Once again, access to more information was what brought Deborah to full time veganism. In fact, Facebook was the turning point for Deborah. She told me she had resisted being on it for years but eventually a friend set it up for her, she got a tablet and suddenly found herself sitting up in bed at night scouring the Internet.

Deborah remembers following a few dog shelter Facebook pages, which led to a pivotal encounter with a post about the Yulin dog festival, and she was horrified. 'At that point, I hadn't made the connection between how we view animals differently. I started to research veganism and make small changes but one day I clicked several links and ended up watching a video of chicks falling from a conveyor belt into a macerator. I was hysterical. I was racked with guilt for all the years I had colluded with the horrific egg industry and I hadn't even explored the dairy industry at that point. That almost tipped me over the edge!'

Deborah made the decision right then and there to live vegan. She stopped buying non-vegan food, started researching vegan alternatives and relentlessly explored the Internet. She joined online groups, read about abolitionist and intersectional politics, and searched for ways to align her new interest in veganism with her beliefs in social justice. All of Deborah's non-vegan clothing was sold on eBay with proceeds donated to Dr Hadwen Trust, a UK-based organisation campaigning for alternatives to animal-based testing. Deborah says, 'It probably took me a year to feel fully vegan but since the day I saw that video and made that decision, I have not knowingly eaten any animal product.'

Three years have passed since Deborah committed to living vegan and in that time I have watched her become more involved in vegan advocacy. She believes that going vegan 'has changed my life totally. It has changed me and the people around me.' Deborah has made dozens of friends since she began passionately supporting animal welfare and even her brother and sister are now vegan while her parents have made a few small changes such as buying plant milk.

Deborah's story ends with a very poignant reflection on remaining compassionate to non-vegans. 'I look at everything differently now and sometimes that is hard to live with. The awareness of how cruel the world is and how determined people are to hold onto old ways is tough to accept, but I have to remember that was me once and I was never a bad person. Even though being vegan can feel overwhelming at times, I surround myself with other compassionate people who understand and it really does lessen the burden.'

I also reached out to one of my favourite people on the planet for insight into why people go and stay vegan. Sonja Ter Horst formed Love Like Hate, an alternative rock band based in Brisbane, Australia, with her partner Heather Cheketri. As a band, they are unapologetically political.

They champion causes near and dear to them, including feminism, veganism and the protection of animals.

Sonja gave me some background into the duo's veganism by saying, 'Heather was raised as a vegetarian and was still meat-free when I met her. I however was vegetarian as a teenager, which was nothing more than a naive alternative fashion trend. I was not vegetarian by the time I was in my twenties.'

About ten years ago, Heather was volunteering for an animal liberation group and having ethical concerns about the dairy industry and one night the pair got talking. Sonja recalls saying that it made no sense to be a vegetarian if your motivation was to protect animals. The conversation centred on the environment and animal cruelty. Heather and Sonja debated why someone would eat something if they didn't have to. That very night they both committed to veganism.

Sonja reflected, 'Back then it was not very common to be vegan in our city. We had vegan friends who lived in rural New South Wales and they gave us a recipe book that set us on the path of trying to make that one food that is a stumbling block for a lot of us. Cheese! We found it wasn't that difficult. It just required a bit more research and creativity in the kitchen to master soured nut cheese. It was not like now where there are ridiculous amounts of alternative food choices for vegans. We were on our own for a lot of the basics we now take for granted.'

So what was the sticking point for Heather and Sonja? How did veganism hold for them?

Heather will be the first to tell anyone who will listen that she is vegan because animal cruelty for her is a black and white, non-negotiable topic. Sonja looks at her veganism more broadly by asking, 'Why would anyone choose to eat something that has so many negative impacts on so many human and animal lives, not to mention the environmental destruction, when they really don't need to?'

So what these stories show, is that there isn't one correct way to get to veganism. However, the common thread is that it took a personal realisation for each and every person in order for them to feel willing and able to commit to a vegan lifestyle. For many of us that have made the commitment to animal-free living, we also have a special person or group of people who gently eased us into our veganism by being friendly and visible, not by shaming us. I often think of how my friend Vanessa had a long-term impact on me and my compassionate awakening and wonder how long it would have taken me to reach a vegan way of living had my first encounter with a vegetarian been embarrassing and filled with shame.

When you have a deep understanding in your heart of why veganism is a kinder option and you have the means to make those choices (coupled with kind yet persistent voices to move you along), it becomes a pivotal turning point in your life and I rarely meet a person who comes back from that place.

Recharge and Refuel

Popcorn is one of my favourite snacks, mainly due to the fact you can flavour it in an unlimited number of ways. My special go-to recipe involves taking three tablespoons of nutritional yeast, your desired amount of Himalayan pink salt and a solid shake of ground chipotle chilli powder. Don't go overboard with the chipotle if you are not used to it. Grind the three dry ingredients into a fine powder in either a spice grinder or pestle and mortar before sprinkling liberally over freshly cooked hot popcorn. You'll be in spicy cheesy popcorn heaven.

CHAPTER TWO
VEGAN 101

> Using animals for food, clothing and entertainment
> at the expense of their freedom and comfort is an
> established way of the world that takes a lot of work
> to dismantle.

The previous chapter was a little heavy going with all
the emotional revelations and personal growth you were
expected to digest. Reducing animal suffering isn't a light-
hearted or laughing matter (although I do know my fair
share of vegan stand up comedians, but that's a book full
of tofu jokes for another time) but I'll try to take it a little
easier on you for this next instalment as I break down what
living vegan actually means.

This chapter is all about those vegan basics. The everyday scenarios you find yourself in as a vegan can often be part of a frightening unknown that holds people back from making the plant-based shift. Even for individuals with a clear and defined understanding of how their choices impact animals, the day to day logistics of living as a vegan can seem insurmountable.

Of course, I'm not going to dismiss the gravity of choosing vegan and what that means to your everyday life but I'm hoping that by presenting the realities of going vegan into bite-sized, digestible chunks, the task of moving toward a life free of animal products will seem less daunting and more doable.

In this chapter, I will take you on a rollicking journey through the world of veganism. It will be a wild ride, taking in the history of the vegan movement, what choices you will make as a vegan, and some bread and butter-less facts about what it means to choose this compassionate path. You'll no doubt have a number of your own questions that you will want answering, so I'll try my best to give you a broad overview of what living vegan means and hopefully your concerns and queries will fall somewhere within the parameters. I'm a one-size-fits-all kind of Fat Gay Vegan!

SO, YOU WANT TO KNOW ABOUT VEGANISM?

Everyone wants a piece of veganism. I can't leave the house without random strangers demanding to know the intricacies of eking out a vegan existence in this mixed up world. What does 'vegan' mean? What can you eat? Is it true that Beyoncé/Morrissey/Bill Clinton is vegan? How can you be fat and be a vegan? Can you eat eggs/fish/honey? Don't you ever just sneak a piece of cheese? What would you do if you were stranded on a desert island with only a pig and a barbecue?

Mainstream newspapers and clickbait websites are rammed solid with stories of celebrities trying their hand at plant-based living, reporters going vegan for 30 days, and all manner of half-baked references to animal-free options. Search engine statistics would have us believe 'vegan' is breaking the Internet daily. However, you might find it surprising to discover that much of this plant-based media saturation actually fails to effectively convey the true meaning of the 'V' word.

It's no wonder people are often confused when they first decide to explore living vegan. There is a great deal of misinformation or watering down of veganism as a term, leading people to not quite understand what it is all about. When Beyoncé is seen walking out of a vegan restaurant one week but is then photographed wearing fur the next, or Bill Clinton tells us he is vegan apart from the fish he eats, there is a danger that these mixed messages will dilute the strength of what vegan means.

When people ask me for a definition of veganism, I usually fall back on my stock response of explaining it as a lifestyle choice concerned with reducing harm to animals by lessening our dependence on them as commodities. This is often met by, 'What the heck are you going on about?'

Put simply, a vegan works hard to avoid buying, eating, wearing, or exploiting animals to the best of their ability.

In the interest of supplying you with a vegan definition that will work for you in the real world, I asked a few people I know and admire to share their take on the meaning of veganism. If my explanation doesn't float your boat, perhaps one of these compassionate and clever people will have what you need.

A reward of listening to and sharing vegan stories is the rich tapestry of human experiences you encounter. Since I started writing my blog, I have met countless inspirational people and enjoyed hearing personal stories from all across the planet. I have marvelled at the dedication shown by small business owners, the dizzying success of vegan CEOs, and the humbling newfound sense of determination shown by new vegans. Taking the time to listen to these perspectives of veganism from everyone from activists to people you casually bump into is often just the fuel you need to fire up your own approach to living vegan. There is inspiration everywhere.

LOUISE WALLIS is a hero to a lot of people and with good reason. I could fill a book on Louise and her outstanding commitments to improving outcomes for animals. She is the founder of World Vegan Day, a celebration marked all over the planet on 1 November each year. Louise created this internationally recognised day during her time as director of The Vegan Society and the accomplished writer, musician and DJ (I'm worn out by everything she does!) now dedicates her energies into running a vegan bar, restaurant and live music venue in north London called Kabaret at Karamel with her partner Frank Hutson.

'Veganism is living without exploiting animals. In practice, it means not consuming products derived from or tested on animals. Start with your diet as a baseline and take it from there. I've always seen veganism as direct action. By boycotting cruel industries and practices, and using your spending power on kinder alternatives you are creating change every day. You're challenging the commodification of animals and showing that there is another way, one that brings considerable benefits for humans too.

'Veganism isn't just about consumer choices. It's a movement representing the rights of animals, who have no voice or power of their own. Being vegan means being an advocate for animals and advancing their cause in whatever way feels right for you. This might be through campaigning, running cookery classes, writing books, blogging, designing fashion, or creating art, poetry or music. The possibilities are endless and people just need to find their strength.'

Being vegan and living a vegan life is not a cookie cutter situation. There is no pre-determined way to arrive at veganism and each person will have their own feelings about how and why they make the commitment. Similarly, once you have decided that a vegan lifestyle is in your future you might also want to explore how you present or champion that decision to the world. As Louise explained, there is close to a limitless number of ways of making veganism a worthwhile and celebrated part of your life.

For a lot of people, the decision to live vegan is something of which they are extremely proud and it means a whole lot to them to be able to share it with the world. Often vegans like to express their commitment by becoming further involved in activism, organising social events, promoting films about animal protection, and even finding lines of employment that complement the care they exhibit for non-human animals.

DEMETRIUS BAGLEY is a fabulous person and someone who is worth looking up when you start your vegan journey. He is bursting with compassion for animals and enthusiasm for promoting veganism. Demetrius wears so many hats that it's tough for me to narrow down my praises, but I suppose I will go with what gives the best representation of his interests and achievements. Demetrius is an award-winning movie producer behind the world-changing documentary *Vegucated*, an events producer involved with some of the biggest plant-based festivals in the USA, one of the voices behind Vegan Travel Club and, because he has so much spare time, he is also an astrologer.

'Veganism for me is about consciously choosing what we're connecting with to maximize peace for all life – the Earth, the animals, and humans, including our self. It is about being less harmful all around.'

The more compact a definition of veganism is, the more powerful and persuasive I believe it becomes. We live in a world where we have become accustomed to only consuming news and views in blink-and-you'll-miss-it pieces. Of course there is space for long explanations and in-depth studies of the why and how of veganism (take this book as a lengthy example), but I'm always secretly pleased to hear a person explain their ethical approach to caring for animals with one or two sentences. You just have to have a way to reach people in a hurry in this day and age. After all, life can sometimes feel like one big YouTube video and everyone has their finger hovering over the 'skip ad' button.

MARIANA BLANCO is a force to be reckoned with in the Mexico City vegan scene. As I sat down to write this chapter, Mariana was deep into the fifth anniversary celebrations for her vegan food business called Los Loosers. This food delivery service was launched back in 2012 with a definite DIY approach. From a tiny kitchen in one of the biggest cities on the planet, Mariana has built Los Loosers into a world famous brand and has cooked for numerous Mexican and international celebrities, as well as travelling to Tokyo by invitation in order to present her unique cuisine to the Japanese public.

'For me, being vegan means being brave enough to have congruency between your thoughts and your actions. It is about living up to your own standards and expectations and by being completely in control of you. You can successfully adopt a vegan lifestyle by transforming yourself. Being vegan is not only about avoiding animal cruelty, it also means being satisfied and content with your personal choices.'

It is completely OK to be feeling a tad overwhelmed by a bunch of long-term vegans telling you what they think and how righteous veganism is. It is important as a new or future vegan to reach out to friends with a foot in both the vegan and non-vegan worlds to give you some insights that might be a little bit more relatable to your journey right now.

I admit to being guilty of not always being able to connect with yet-to-be vegans as effectively as I could. The vegan journey does change how you look at the world and it is always easier to connect or relate to people who are living a similar reality. An important piece of advice I would give to any newbies on the vegan scene is to look for people in a similar situation to you. That might mean someone who has been vegan for a similar amount of time as you, it might mean a person with a similar home life, or you might find yourself making friends with someone with whom you can make the vegan transition with together.

> **iVáN BUSTiLLOS** is someone who has developed a stronger interest in veganism the longer we have been friends, although of course I am not trying to take credit for his compassionate awakening! Iván lives in Mexico City (with his boyfriend and two cats) where he has worked as an industrial engineer after relocating from the northern Mexican state of Chihuahua in 2013. He now has access to a whole new world of vegan restaurants, stores and experiences in the capital and has identified as vegan for six months at the time of writing this book.
>
> 'Veganism for me is as simple as one word. Respect. What I believe to be the core argument of veganism is the universal idea that all living creatures deserve to be respected and have a chance to experience life as free as possible. Foremost, us as humans and conscious beings have the ultimate responsibility to respect and protect the rest of the living creatures within our environment starting with the fundamental act of not ending their lives for selfish and egocentric purposes.

'I became vegan because I got to a point where it was unbearable to think that my eating habits cost the lives of innocent creatures. I might say that it all started out as guilt and quickly evolved into the idea of becoming part of the change by the simple act of making different lifestyle choices. I would like to explore veganism further because I consider it an integral part of my lifestyle and of course I like discovering food all over again!'

Now you have a few definitions of the term vegan from seasoned plant-eaters and recent animal-free lifestylers on which to reflect. Not only did I want to share their compassionate thoughts in order to help the newly-vegan amongst us, but to also show you how powerful it can be to have a clear idea of what vegan means to you. Having a definite understanding of why you are choosing to live as a vegan actually makes the journey or transition to veganism a whole lot easier. When you have that definition or terminology in your head and in your heart, there is no looking back and you will be well-armed for all future 'but bacon' jokesters and resistant (or antagonistic?) relatives.

THE STORY OF 'VEGAN'

From where on earth does the word originate? To explore the history of the word and term 'vegan', I had no other choice but to turn to the organisation at the centre of it all.

Let's get acquainted with The Vegan Society and find out what they have to say about it.

The Vegan Society was founded in the UK in 1944 when Donald Watson and a group of fellow non-dairy vegetarians coined the term 'vegan' by taking the beginning and the end of the word vegetarian in order to better represent the choices they were making around animals. They were trying to draw a distinct line in the sand between what we now commonly refer to as vegan and people who reject meat but still might consume eggs, cheese and milk.

In the decades since the formation of The Vegan Society and the word vegan itself, the organisation has grown into one of the best-known animal advocacy groups on the planet. Based in Birmingham in the middle of England, The Vegan Society is now probably most famous for their vegan trademark scheme that involves companies licensing a small logo from the Society to indicate that a product is suitable for vegans. It is instantly recognisable for consumers looking to omit animal products (or animal testing) from their shopping list and the Society now supplies this vegan validation to thousands of products every year. The trademark scheme also gives businesses a direct line to plant-based shoppers who can scan supermarket shelves for the distinct flower trademark logo.

However, The Vegan Society isn't just about putting a logo onto a few packets of animal-free sausages. An entire web of support and information services spring forth from the work they do, including lobbying governments, public awareness campaigns, support services for new and established vegans, wellbeing advice and a sizeable well of resources including recipes, meal ideas, lists of vegan businesses and even real-life people you can contact if you want vegan friends or acquaintances.

It seemed sensible to ask the Society if they stand by one simple definition of what being vegan means. Their explanation is concise and surely the benchmark when it comes to describing veganism: 'Veganism is a way of living which seeks to exclude, as far as is possible and practicable, all forms of exploitation of, and cruelty to, animals for food, clothing or any other purpose.'

Leave it to The Vegan Society to have formed the definitive explanation of veganism. It sure is a lot stronger and far more compelling than mine.

While the word vegan can be traced back to the 1940s, the idea of people protecting the interests of animals by not eating, wearing or exploiting them goes back a lot further into human history than Mr Watson and his merry band of non-dairy vegetarians.

My friend **DR IAN MCDONALD** recently made a radio series titled *The History of Vegetarianism* in which he searched for the origins of what a lot of modern humans think of as veganism.

'Even though there wasn't a word for it until 1944, the idea that it's wrong to eat animals and it's wrong to eat animal products has been around as long as organised vegetarianism.

'Indian vegetarianism has, for millennia, treated eggs (but not milk) as meat. From the decline of Rome to medieval China, a sacred order called the Elect of the Manichaeans (a lost world religion) followed a vegan diet because their rituals required them to live an utterly pure life – and they recognised the violence of milk and eggs. When western vegetarianism got organised in the 1840s, the people who came up with the word "vegetarian" were living in a "vegan" commune in west London.

'And from then on, whenever vegetarians communicate, there's usually someone suggesting that milk and eggs can't really be vegetarian. Early twentieth century France even boasted an anarchist vegan movement called *les végétaliens*. But this doesn't get organised until 1944. After a series of letters in the vegetarian magazine, and trouncing the lacto-ovo-vegetarians in a debate in Croydon, half-a-dozen "non-dairy vegetarians" met in a feminist veggie food club within sight of the British Museum on 5 November 1944.

'Various names were thrown around, including "Allvega" – possibly inspired by The Vega, the poshest veggie café in London at the time, set up by a socialist German couple who'd fled the Nazis. The organiser, a pacifist woodwork teacher called Donald Watson, leaned towards "vegan", and no one came up with a better name.

'Donald Watson ran the whole thing himself for a couple of years, including the quarterly newsletter, before The Vegan Society could be properly set up and others could take over. And that magazine is still published quarterly by The Vegan Society today.'

Like any social justice or anti-oppression movement of which you find yourself a part, you have so much to personally gain by exploring where the basic underpinning principles powering that movement came from. Knowing the history of the people who championed animal rights before you might just be the inspiration you need on your journey.

WHERE DO i STaRT?

So we've had our history lesson and we're ready with the language to describe what vegan means when the need arises, but what does reducing your reliance on animal products actually mean on a day-to-day basis? As we have heard above, veganism is about doing the best you can for animals to the best of your ability and within your means, so let's explore some of the common situations in which you might find yourself as a person trying to reduce harm and suffering to non-human animals.

First and foremost, you can change your eating habits. Simple and obvious, right? Our modern take on food production unfortunately results in the cruel treatment and grisly deaths of a staggering number of cows, chickens, pigs and many other animals. As a person who has decided to take action for animals, the easiest and simplest way to approach the problem is to stop eating them. This step is surprisingly simple yet shockingly effective, and it will change your entire outlook on how you interact with the world around you. You still get to eat delicious food while reducing your contribution to suffering. It's a win-win situation.

As with a lot of things in life, capitalism got cosy with its old friends supply and demand and now we have an endless supply of plant-based food alternatives that people in big cities at least can access relatively in line with the cost of non-vegan food. Big brands making convenience food and pantry items are springing up all over the planet and this is resulting in accessible, lower cost options for vegan shoppers. It's true that a lot of meat and dairy replacements can still be pricey at times, but affordable animal-free meal options are becoming increasingly available.

If you have money to spare, decadent recipes featuring cashew and almond cheese will help you completely forget dairy cheese, while you'll likely find jackfruit, seitan and tofu to be useful transitional foods as you move away from animal protein (i.e. flesh). Some of these will even become new foods for life in your home and you'll ponder how you ever existed prior to marinated tempeh.

These days of course, there are loads on the market, but, you will never have to buy a vegan recipe book if you don't want to, or don't have the means to, due to the unfathomable amount of plant-based cooking blogs now saturating the Internet. You can also contact The Vegan Society and groups like Viva! for free recipe and food idea booklets.

As a self-identified junk food fanatic, I'm probably not the best person to be giving out nutritional advice, but suffice to say that it's entirely possible to eat a nutrient-rich, balanced diet as a vegan, despite what some non-vegans would have you believe. If you're worried about obtaining sufficient nutrients, you'll be able to find information on how a human body can get everything it needs while eating vegan, again on sites like The Vegan Society and Viva!. Some vegans choose to take B12 and iodine supplements, among other things, but it's important to do your own research based on your own diet and needs and make well-informed decisions based on trustworthy advice.

So there is a plethora of vegan foodstuffs on the market, endless vegan recipes to try, and instructions and inspiration on how to prepare plant-based food. Your biggest challenge might just be deciding what you want to eat first, and also where you should buy it.

From Sydney to Shanghai, you'll find supermarkets stocked with vegan frozen meals, chicken-less nuggets and egg-free mayonnaise. In the West, if you have the money to spend, you'll find that vegans are being increasingly being well-catered for in mainstream stores. However, it's not only feasible to adopt a plant-based diet if you have a disposable income. There are many organisations and social activist groups around the world who are helping to educate people on how to access plant-based whole foods at affordable prices. As well as enabling people to choose a lifestyle that reduces animal suffering, this can also help communities take control of their nutrient intake, self-manage and improve personal wellbeing while discovering how they can survive and thrive on plant-based foods.

We'll look more at this in chapter four, but for the moment, suffice to say that there are a mind-boggling number of guides to affordable and accessible vegan eating, shopping and cooking. We should remember that eating vegan can be accessible to a lot of people, but only if we work hard to demand equitable access to food, produce and information.

If switching to vegan eating means more to you than just 'no meat and no dairy' (and I think it really should), you will want to get yourself acquainted with hidden animal-derived ingredients. Due to the greed of big business, if there is a tiny piece of an animal remaining following its initial date with an abattoir you can rest assured it will be added to something you will eat, drink or even wear.

Animals and their remains are everywhere.

Here are some examples of the main offenders:

COCHINEAL/CARMINE – a bright red food and drink colouring made from crushed scale insects. Also sometimes listed as carminic acid, Natural Red 4 or

E120, it's used in fruit juices, yogurts, confectionery and many other foodstuffs, as well as added to some blushers and lipsticks.

GELATIN OR GELATINE – a collagen stabiliser derived from rendered animal bones and remains often used in sweets and candy, sodas and soft drinks, some long-life fruit juices, and too many other consumables to list.

LANOLIN – a waxy secretion which is the by-product of sheep or other animal shearing that occasionally ends up in food but more likely in cosmetics, particularly moisturisers, lip balms and mascaras.

VITAMIN D – some vitamin D supplements and additives are made from animal products. D2 is plant-derived but D3 can often be extracted from lanolin.

WAX – many supermarket-stocked fruits around the world are treated with wax before being put on shelves and often this wax is animal-derived, often from bugs, beetles and insects.

And … guess what? I actually don't want to type this list anymore. It's kind of disgusting, right?

Although, there is just one further thing I should mention. Honey. This is the cause of much confusion, and something that non-vegans seem to get oddly hung up on. On the simplest level, vegans do not eat or use any product derived from animals, and beekeepers of course remove the food that the bees have made for themselves for human consumption. In addition, common practices around commercial bee-keeping include the killing of hives in winter to save money during non-production months. Even if the hive is not destroyed, the honey taken is replaced by a sugary water, a poor substitute which the bees then have to try to survive on over the winter. Some beekeepers also clip the wings of the queen to stop the bees from swarming. Honey is a widespread additive to a surprising number of foodstuffs, despite there being a number of plant-based alternatives available.

There are countless resources online showing you how to avoid inadvertently buying products made with animal-derived ingredients. Many activist and vegan support groups publish booklets highlighting hidden ingredients, helping you make on the spot decisions about what you will or won't invest your money on. My partner and I have carried around a credit card-sized guide to 'E' numbers and hidden animal ingredients for years and it has helped us out on many of occasions. It even stopped me from once buying pretzels containing a dough improver called L-cysteine often made from crushed chicken or duck feathers.

If you are unsure, 'E' numbers are codes that are used to refer to specific permitted food additives. The 'E' refers to the European Union, as it is the European Food Safety Authority who approves the additives for use. Outside of the EU, 'E' numbers are used on packaging in a number of other countries including Australia, New Zealand, the Arab Gulf States and Israel, but currently not usually in the US. Not all E numbers are animal derived – and some even might be seen as beneficial, for example, E300 is vitamin C – but some are, so it's worth investigating the number of resources available that can help you easily identify what to avoid.

So that should give you a bit of insight into how the food industry is happy to use all sorts of products derived from animals without necessarily announcing it on the packaging. In addition to this, compassionate shoppers will also want to consider what they are wearing and how animals might be affected by their clothing choices.

If you think buying new leather shoes is passable because the cow/snake/crocodile was already dead, think again my compassionate friend. Animal leathers for clothing and footwear drive up demand for more creatures to be produced faster and cheaper. Leather also works to subsidise the meat and dairy industries, due to the fact that killing animals for food on a mass scale is not actually that cost efficient.

But be aware that even shoes that are not made from leather can use glues or dyes made from animals. If you have the funds available, compassionate footwear can be bought online and spirited to you pretty much anywhere on the planet from retailers such as Moo Shoes in New York City and The Third Estate in London. You will now find even big name brands labelling which of their styles of sneakers are suitable for vegans. I've been into vegan shoe stores in Melbourne, Paris and Portland.

Vegans avoid buying garments made from wool, silk, skin, feathers or anything at all that used to belong to an animal. Look for linen over wool, satin over silk, and absolutely anything over fur. Every single item that you buy that has been made using animal skin or feathers means that at least one animal has suffered and/or died for that item to come into being. If there is an alternative and you can afford to, buy it; do it for the animals.

Many new vegans ask me and other old timers what they should do with old clothing and footwear once they become vegan. Nobody can answer this question and stand by it except you. But since you asked my opinion, if you can afford to replace your wardrobe with one hundred per cent vegan items overnight you are probably an extremely privileged and wealthy human and you should buy a truckload of this book to distribute around the planet.

For the rest of us with slightly less extravagant means, we are more likely to accept the financial reality of the situation and commit to replacing non-vegan with vegan when the former wears out. I would probably make an exception with a 12-foot feather boa or an alligator-skin flat cap. These things are not only noticeably animal but they can in no way be deemed crucial to your ongoing happiness. You need shoes to go to work, however you don't need alligator anything to leave the house.

You can take your veganism to the next level by committing to buying and using personal care and hygiene products that do not contain animal-derived ingredients and that were not tested on animals. There have been huge advancements in this area over the past few years and I can now tidy myself up with vegan versions of toothpaste, shampoo, body wash, styling cream and hairspray. Some major personal product chains around the world, such as Sally Beauty and Superdrug, stock a wide range of items labelled as suitable for vegans.

Just as vegan personal products can now be found in increasing numbers, so too can household cleaning and maintenance products (in certain parts of the world). In my experience, this is the part of living vegan that is easiest in the UK. I've been in Mexican towns and cities where there is not one box of vegan-certified washing detergent to be found anywhere. As I love sounding like a broken record, I'll say it again. Do what you can when you can. Look for alternatives and use them when you can find them. If you are travelling, take small amounts of what you think you will need. This not only rescues you from having to buy non-vegan alternatives, it also cuts down on waste related to buying something of which you will only use a fraction.

This next part sounds simple on the surface, but there is a tricky part to it. As a vegan, you will want to stay away from industries and entertainment that exploit animals. Zoos, aquatic parks, circuses, horse racing, dog racing, state fairs, and even theme parks all put animals to work for human entertainment. Being vegan not only means resisting the urge or expectation to visit these establishments, but to also navigate social situations during which friends and family members expect you to partake. You get better with time at these tricky interactions. Honesty is the best policy and you can't go wrong when delivering your point of view about animals in entertainment with a kind assertion that it is simply something you don't support.

If you believe in and stand by your decision to live vegan, there is no social situation you can't manage effectively and sensitively. I've been faced with the task of telling the parents of my students that I didn't want the chocolate, cheese and wine their children were giving me at the end of the school year. If you're honest and open, in my experience, people are sensitive and understanding more often than not.

Medication causes concern for vegans. We go to a lot of trouble to remove dependence on animals from all parts of our lives but then the doctor wants to give us medicine or treatment containing animal-derived ingredients. This is one of those times I would recommend you ask to look over several options available to you and pick the version of the medicine you feel comfortable with as a vegan. People need medicine to stay well, control illness, manage mental wellbeing, prolong time with loved ones, and for an un-listable number of reasons.

Most medicines have been tested on animals and this is close to impossible to avoid. Give yourself a break around medicine. Do what you can, take medicines and treatments that you need and don't punish yourself emotionally over it. If this is an area of great concern for you, get involved by supporting charities such as Animal Free Research UK, which works to champion alternatives to animal-based laboratory testing. We live in a system that has made it virtually impossible to avoid animal ingredients in medicine and you can only do your best while looking after your wellbeing.

One fabulous thing about learning to live vegan is the fact that so many people have been there before you and you do not have to reinvent the wheel. Resources are everywhere and they are your friends. You might find yourself overwhelmed by discovering that a sizeable number of alcoholic drinks such as wine and beer are not suitable for vegans, however drinks database Barnivore takes the stress out of a night on the town. The website is searchable for breweries, wine producers and drink companies all over the planet and contains user-collected information to help you discover what is vegan at your local watering hole.

Happycow is the most well-known and widely accessed English language web resource for vegan and vegetarian restaurants and the app version can help you out of a lot of sticky situations on the road. Todo Vegano is the definitive resource for vegan listings in Latin America, even including in depth information about vegan businesses in cities across the USA with sizeable Latino/a communities. If you don't speak or read Spanish, there's an English language version of the site, that includes all the same information.

If you are curious about what vegan food, products or services you can find in your local area I'd feel fairly confident someone has written about your choices already and if they haven't, you now have a new hobby. Take a moment to get acquainted with some of my favourite online resources at the end of the book. Most large cities and towns now have a Facebook group that you can join in order to connect with local compassionate people and hear about the best places in your area.

Vegans Can Have Non-Vegan Friends

One of the biggest sources of anxiety for new vegans or those considering it, is the prospect of having to go to dinner with meat-eating friends. Social conditioning is strong on this one and a lot of us dread the idea of being different, appearing difficult, causing a scene or any of the number of descriptors thrown at vegans. Hey, we are difficult for an extremely solid reason. We don't want to contribute to suffering.

The good news is that mainstream restaurants around the globe are waking up to the money-making ways of vegan food provision and it is becoming increasingly common to find vegan options being touted by chain eateries, if not entire stand-alone vegan menus. I have marvelled at the vegan menu at a pizza restaurant inside a casino in Las Vegas, ordering almost everything on the menu out of the sheer delight of having so many options in such an unlikely setting. Sandwich shops are rapidly increasing their plant-based offerings while even pubs throughout the UK are keen to trumpet their vegan menus.

Heck, I even once saw a steakhouse on one of my travels with a chalkboard on the front steps advertising the vegan special of the day.

Speaking up as a vegan in a social setting can take a little getting used to and might just be the aspect of veganism you find the most daunting, especially when you are surrounded by people who believe eating factory-farmed animals is an acceptable way to exist. Our friends, families and colleagues are important when it comes to feeling we are loved and appreciated humans, so our social interactions with them is valuable to us and we don't like to see that threatened. This is where these mainstream restaurants with vegan-friendly menus come into their own. There probably will be times in your life where you feel you can't get out of that particular birthday party, work celebration or family gathering (or perhaps you even WANT to attend!) and this is where a non-vegan pizza restaurant with a vegan menu can come in. Knowing the chain restaurants that can accommodate you will help you navigate the social requirements while staying true to your animal free lifestyle, so you can enjoy the company of people who like you and make you feel special.

Allowing yourself to dip in and out of non-vegan establishments willing to serve you vegan food doesn't mean you should forget about businesses that have put themselves on the line by dedicating their lives to operating completely devoid of animal products. Historically, the one hundred per cent vegan businesses have tended to be more expensive than their meat and dairy riddled competition but this is clearly due to supply and demand economics. Prices come down when a lot of people want something and suppliers can sell in bulk, so with the increased interest in plant-based eating we are seeing a corresponding drop in the cost of vegan items. In addition, a lot of animal-based industry and commerce is heavily subsidised by governments the world over. Meat and dairy is cheap because it can be everywhere thanks to this financial support.

Shop with vegan businesses when you can afford it and when you have the time. The survival of a lot of these places depends on the support of local people just like you. Yes, you have the power to keep the doors open and the bills paid. It might mean stopping in at an independent vegan grocer as well as the big business supermarket in order to get the weekly shopping list completely filled, but you will be supporting small businesses who are in the business of improving outcomes for animals.

If you ever find yourself struggling to match your belief in veganism with your personal life, get involved. Support causes that promote veganism, attend vegan events and make vegan friends. Chapter five explores in more detail the benefit of community, but I will say briefly that community doesn't just mean going along to a vegan drinks event to make friends once a month (although that is awesome fun and can be an important part of being happy). Contributing with your time, enthusiasm and money if you have it is a sure-fire way to feel celebrated and confident in your veganism. You are part of a movement doing fabulous things to help people, the planet and animals.

When it comes to interpersonal relationships with non-vegans, there are a few basic rules of play I always recommend when asked.

There is a fairly solid chance if you are reading this book you were not vegan at some point in your life. Most of us were not born or raised vegan and the journey to grow into our compassion takes time and space to explore our new understandings. This should be at the front of your mind when dealing with loved ones, family members, friends and colleagues. Cast your mind back to before you were vegan (or maybe you are almost there right now) and remember how fundamentally you were socialised into believing animals were yours to consume, wear and clap at while they jumped through hoops.

Using animals for food, clothing and entertainment at the expense of their freedom and comfort is an established way of the world that takes a lot of work to dismantle.

I'm not suggesting you throw yourself at the mercy of bacon pranksters and the protein curious by being a gentle, kind vegan all the time. Just as you need to do with other personal choices in your life, put your pleather boot down firm when you need to assert yourself. Use unwavering resolve with friends and family when describing your vegan choices and let them know what their support and understanding means to you. Offer to cook for or contribute to group meals, be insistent yet kind in your assertion for the reasons behind your veganism and be a powerful advocate for animals by standing by what you believe in.

It's totally OK not to take a food or drink offering that isn't vegan. If people love and care for you, they will be fine with your choices – even if they're slightly baffled by some of them. Using animals whenever you want is a tough framework to dismantle down and you are at the forefront of the battle.

*

There is a lot of information to take in from this chapter we are just finishing up. The basic take away from all this can be broken down to the fact if you do what you can you are helping animals. You are making a very real and tangible statement every time you choose NOT TO eat meat, eat dairy, drink non-vegan beer, go to the circus, buy from a dog breeder, attend a theme park showcasing animals, buy non-vegan cosmetics, or use non-vegan cleaning products. You are actively and effectively lessening the demand for animal derived products and ingredients. Your consumer activism is a trend that is shaping how big business sees and uses animals for monetary gain.

Even though supporting multinational companies and conglomerates is not the goal (more on that later), many of us have limited options when it comes to where we shop and we mostly learn to live vegan within a capitalist society. How we choose to consume within this system has a far-reaching impact and how you present yourself as a vegan to those around you has the power to open ears, eyes, hearts and minds.

Recharge and Refuel

By the time you read this book, jackfruit will have well and truly jumped the shark, but it is such an incredible food that it deserves special mention here.

Grab a tin or two of the young green jackfruit in brine, rinse it, chop off the hard parts if you fancy and start cooking in a pan with ANY combination of flavours. The more flavours the better. Heck, I've even cooked it in ketchup and some sea salt and it has come out of the pan soft, tasty and so very versatile.

Top tip: oven-roast the cooked jackfruit at a high temperature until you really start to get a chewy consistency you'll adore.

CHAPTER THREE

VEGAN MEANS VEGAN

> Victories for animals come faster and more assuredly
> when we spread our unwavering message with a
> kind conviction.

If you first heard about veganism via mainstream media or
social networking platforms during the past five years or so,
there is a solid chance the term has been presented to you
alongside weight reduction or physical wellness messages.
Magazines feature top ten lists of vegan celebrities and

exclusive reports on how vegan living can make your body better, skin brighter or life longer. Of course, people can live a vegan lifestyle and make personal choices about their own wellness, but it is important for the effectiveness of the vegan message that it doesn't become diluted or conflated with other definitions or motivations.

Vegan means one thing and, as we explored early on in this book, that one thing is improving outcomes for non-human animals through the choices we make about what we eat, wear and use. Veganism is not a diet. Try to tell a vegan their choices are a diet and we might very well slap you with a wet slab of tofu. Being vegan is a choice that affects all aspects of your life including the stuff that goes into your mouth, but it is about so much more than just food. To sell veganism as a dietary control tool or skin improvement regime is to do it a grave injustice. This approach works to perpetuate negative stereotypes and damaging, unrealistic standards about body shape and size.

When weight loss is conflated with veganism, it falls into the dangerous area of body shaming and misogyny. Mainstream media loves to make women feel inferior when it comes to their bodies and unfortunately veganism has recently become another weapon in this sexist war on our society. Thin white women are used to sell veganism as a quick fix to a more desirable body at the expense of anyone who doesn't fit the cookie cutter idea of female perfection. In addition, these images and messages work to oppress women of colour and people living with disabilities. Selling veganism as anything other than caring for animals often leads to oppression, plain and simple. We need to resist this approach to promoting veganism by drawing the fight back to animals. Every single time.

Despite our longstanding reputation as tree huggers of the highest order, veganism is not about environmentalism at its core. Of course all humans should be concerned about protecting our natural world, and eating a plant-based diet can have an incredibly positive impact on our planet. Protecting the environment is one hell of a bonus of adopting a vegan lifestyle, although, because I love sounding like a broken record, I must reiterate that it is not the main motivation or meaning behind the word and concept.

I won't bore you with all of the facts and figures but it is becoming impossible to ignore the fact that modern animal agriculture is the largest contributor to greenhouse emissions on the planet. The United Nations' *Livestock's Long Shadow: Environmental Issues and Options* report suggested that the negative impacts of animal agriculture and industrialised farming need to be addressed urgently to counteract long-lasting environmental degradation.

Our planet is warming at record rates and cutting out our dependency on large land mammals for food is one of the most effective ways to tackle this global problem. We can save animals from unnecessary suffering AND do good for our environment.

NO THANKS, I'M VEGAN

There has been a bizarre and somewhat confusing new approach to promoting veganism involving spokespeople and personalities telling people to not 'rock the boat' by standing resolutely in their veganism. By this I mean there are activists who are spreading the message of excusing yourself from being vegan for a brief moment if it is going to cause even slight feelings of discomfort or conflict around friends, family or colleagues. They believe if you ask for the vegan wine list during a night out in a restaurant, politely turn down a pickled egg at the pub, or talk about your new vegan Sketchers during a group spin class you are somehow setting the vegan movement back twenty years or making the lifestyle seem like the most unappealing choice on the planet.

If your grandparents cook you a cake but forget about the animal ingredients part of your lifestyle choice, these activists believe it is in the best interest of animals to quietly and politely accept a slice and eat it. They don't want you to shove the egg-laden carrot cake back at your grandparents like an ungrateful brat. Another example given by these apologetic vegans involves beer. They believe that if you attend a party and are offered a beer, you should accept it and drink it without considering if it has been filtered with the use of swim bladders from fish who were minding their own business. They believe it is in the best interests of veganism that you don't take a minute to check a vegan brands app on your phone and you don't mention to any partygoer within earshot that you prefer your beer without animal by-products.

These vegan activists would have us believe that by speaking up about veganism or politely turning down a food or drinking offering because it is not vegan will somehow make veganism look uncool or completely unattainable. They think if you don't eat the non-vegan cake, you are going to be building a barrier between your grandparents and their possible conversion to a plant-based life. Somehow the people at the party will forever remember you not taking that non-vegan beer and they will laugh until the end of their days about the combative and difficult vegan while they guzzle bacon flavoured beer.

I absolutely disagree with this approach. Staying true to your beliefs and asserting your veganism is crucial for many reasons.

Firstly, explaining your veganism to friends and family helps to reinforce your commitment to living more compassionately. Situations in which you talk other people through your reasons for being vegan are great for helping you understand and appreciate how exactly your choices are helping to improve outcomes for animals. The more comfortable you become with being able to describe your reasons for living animal free, the more believable and authentic your viewpoints will seem to you and to others. Standing up for your beliefs makes you a better advocate and spokesperson for animals.

You can lead by example by using these opportunities to politely decline non-vegan food as a way to normalise your veganism. It's a form of non-confrontational outreach. There is nothing more powerful, no better advertisement for veganism, than a calm and collected person who is able to explain their stance on protecting animals in a non-confrontational, friendly and accessible way. Use humour and honesty. Your friends and family should want you to be happy and proud of your choices and, by speaking with ease and confidence of veganism, you will be the best advertisement for protecting animals in your part of the planet.

I know what a lot of you are probably thinking right about now, and that's that I sound like I'm full of soy-based baloney. It's one thing for this chubby, hairy guy to preach on these pages about standing up for your veganism in possibly sensitive and emotional situations, but it's doubtful he actually does it for himself in the real world. To put your fears of being duped by my moralising words to rest, here are a few legitimate situations in which I've had to stand firm yet friendly within my veganism.

I mentioned being a schoolteacher previously during an anecdote about my time in the north of England. There were two highlights of the teaching year for me and the main one was the feeling when I finished writing all thirty report cards. After weeks of toiling away, placing those soul-sucking pieces of paper onto the head teacher's desk was beyond liberating. The other best part of the school year was getting presents from the students when it was all over. Yes, I'm greedy for gifts.

The joy of being showered with presents for the first time was only slightly dampened by the fact that the first few gifts I received were not suitable for vegans. I recall some expensive dairy cheese and a box of chocolates finding their way into my desk and I knew instantly that I was going to have to get the word out about my veganism. I didn't want to contribute to animal product consumption by these families spending money on non-vegan gifts, nor did I want to be dishonest by accepting the gifts with a smile on my face.

I waited until I could have a quiet word with the parents and I explained my vegan status. I voiced my genuine appreciation for the kindness their family had shown to me by buying a gift and how I didn't want their hard-earned money to go to waste on a product I wouldn't use. Every single parent and caregiver I spoke with was completely understanding, some even apologetic. Of course I stressed how there was no need for them to feel bad as there was no way of them knowing I was a vegan.

Every gift I received following these conversations was suitable for vegans. Of course, I made it explicitly clear that my favourite brand of whisky was vegan-friendly, resulting in more than a few bottles adorned with ribbons making their way to me. The whole experience of simply saying 'I'm vegan' was eye opening. My young students wanted to know what vegan meant, if my shoes were made from cows, and how they could make links between the food and lifestyle choices made by me and other people they knew. There was no animosity between anyone involved; I got to stand proud and uncompromised in my veganism, and it started multiple conversations in the classroom and I'm certain in a few homes.

My next example of being unapologetically vegan involves a house party I attended in Los Angeles many years ago. This particular party sticks in my mind because the house was at the top of the steepest street in the city (you don't become a Fat Gay Vegan by striding up hillsides) and I got involved in a constructive discussion about vegan beer.

I like to plan ahead for a party by bringing my own beer. Not only do I think it is good form to show up at a party with a few drink contributions, I also don't like finding myself in a situation where there is nothing vegan to drink. I made a commitment to myself a long time ago that if I couldn't confirm the vegan status of a beer and there was nothing else available, I'd go without. To be prepared for this particular house party, I stopped in at the local grocery store before I arrived in order to pick up a carton of vegan-suitable cans.

After slinking into the party in my coolest West Coast manner that was most definitely not cool on reflection, I asked the host if I could deposit my beer in the refrigerator. The host was keen to point out that he had already supplied drinks and I was welcome to help myself. This gave me the opening to briefly discuss my motivation for bringing my own drinks. My host was very surprised to learn that beer may not be vegan due to animal by-products such as fish swim bladders and gelatine used for clarification and was totally open to accepting my choice. In fact, he was so impressed to learn these new facts he proceeded to march around the party to let guests know there was now vegan beer in the fridge if anyone was in need. After all, this was LA and there was no way I was the only plant-based guest in the room.

I had a top time at the party. Not only did I get to meet a bunch of fun people, but I also had the valuable experience of asserting my veganism in a non-threatening manner to a group of accepting people. My decision to speak up to the host opened a dialogue about how beer can sometimes not be animal free and my hope is that the situation planted a seed of thought about how small changes such as the beer we drink at a party can be a simple way for people to explore or expand their compassion. It's an invitation of sorts as much as it's a declaration of my own thoughtful and considered choices.

Every conversation about your veganism is a planted seed of thought and an opportunity to reach non-vegans. If you approach your vegan lifestyle with a true sense of it being the right thing to do, you will be a believable and positive role model. I truly believe it is more effective to be an outspoken and approachable advocate who stands firm in your veganism than a person who looks like they will fold at the first sign of conflict. Be kind to non-vegans, don't shame people for their choices, and stand up for what you believe in. You'll be the best advertisement for the kinder treatment of animals your friends and family have seen.

A few years ago, I was visiting Mexico and had rented short-term accommodation via one of those websites connecting homeowners and tourists. Upon arrival, my host gave me a tour of the property before departing to let me get on with my vacation. After he made himself scarce, I noticed he had left some cheese and snacks in the refrigerator intended for me to enjoy. Of course, it is always lovely to be thought of with gifts but I had no intention of eating any of the non-vegan things supplied by the host. I also can't stand the idea of animal products being thrown in the garbage after individual animals have been involved in the production and I'm not interested in watching people spend money on food that is going to be discarded. I'm not going to eat it but I still understand the concept of waste.

I messaged my host to explain the situation, letting him know that I wouldn't be consuming his gifts even though I was grateful for his kind thoughts. My host was beyond understanding and stopped by shortly after our online interaction to collect the food. He also came armed with a list of nearby vegan recommendations that had been shared with him by friends and previous guests. I had a hard time getting him to leave due to how keen he was to make me feel comfortable about being vegan!

HOW TO TELL iF YOU'Re iN a VeGaN ReSTaURaNT

Restaurants are not vegan if they serve even one animal dish.

As a vegan blogger, I've lost track of how many emails I receive in which a publicist is singing the praises of a new vegan restaurant that turns out not to be vegan. The story usually goes that they are so excited about me discovering the vegan menu and hope I'll want to let the readers of my blog know all about it. I'll pop over to the online menu to find out what all the fuss is about only to be confronted by a list of options that includes eggs, fish, cheese and cream.

When I take the time to respond to these messages and point out that they have mistakenly identified their restaurant as vegan, I am usually told that the owners really want to serve only vegan food but they don't want to make anyone feel excluded. Their desire is to please everyone but focus on plant-based foods. I'm happy to see more vegan options but it is unhelpful to veganism as a movement to claim the word when your restaurant is not vegan.

Veganism is not about allowing a few chicken eggs to slide onto a menu. Veganism is about making a clear and determined distinction between eating and using animal products and not. These restaurants do not get to use the word vegan to describe their business or intentions. By all means they can announce they have options suitable for vegans but they shouldn't be having their publicist or PR firm reaching out to bloggers and media with the message that they are a vegan establishment. It is frankly incorrect and works to diminish the power of the term vegan when newspapers and websites run stories about a new vegan food spot in town and customers turn up to see animal products mixed through the menu.

The same conversation has been part of my life for many years when it comes to restaurants wanting to claim vegan status but still serving hot drinks featuring milk from cows. You are not a vegan establishment if you sell or serve dairy. Not only are non-vegans confused by these mixed messages, the effectiveness of veganism as a label is severely diminished by restaurants trying to use it when they in fact profit from animal exploitation.

i am not 'allergic' to animal products

Veganism does not mean gluten free and it isn't about common allergens, although you might be surprised at how often eating vegan gets conflated with these concepts. Restaurants with wheat free menu items will often include these on the same list as vegan-suitable foods even though the vegan dishes are not necessarily free of animal products and vice-versa.

This framing of veganism as an allergy works to diminish the true message of why we choose this lifestyle. When I am asked what I can or can't eat as a vegan, I always respond by saying I can eat whatever the heck I want but I choose not to eat anything derived from an animal. Some people are required to avoid certain ingredients and foods because they can have negative or dangerous implications for their wellbeing, whereas a vegan chooses to opt out of consuming animal products for external reasons. I do not have a condition or disease that stops me from eating specific foods, but many people do and it is not helpful or kind to lump their needs in with veganism.

There have been calls by some in the retail and catering industries throughout the UK to not allow the labelling of foods as vegan suitable if they have been made in the same factory as foods containing animal derived ingredients and common allergens. This is an example of once again conflating veganism with health issues and considerations. They are not the same thing and shouldn't be lumped together. There is already enough confusion about common allergens and their effects without lumping them in with people opting out of the consumption of animals.

Veganism is about an intention and how we carry that intention out to the best of our abilities. If your favourite pack of plant-based biscuits is made in a factory that also produces other products containing milk and eggs, they are still vegan as long as they do not contain any purposively included animal ingredients. Food allergies are an extremely serious business and manufacturers are bound legally to declare even the most miniscule risk of cross-contamination. Most of the foods you buy with no purposely included animal ingredients will still carry a warning of the possibility of cross contamination. Use your judgement, check online, and learn to be at peace with the idea that you are doing the best you can.

IT'S NOT VEGAN TO 'REDUCE' THE ANIMAL PRODUCTS YOU EAT

Time to get a little more controversial as I ask you to consider the reducetarianism movement and how I believe it shouldn't be promoted by vegan activists. Reducetarianism isn't my attempt to coin up the most ridiculous term I could imagine, but is used to describe when people reduce how many animal products they consume via campaigns such as Meat Free Monday and is often championed as a gateway to veganism. However, the main problem with the concept is that it takes the focus off improving outcomes for animals and instead asks people to consider how their choices contribute to environmental destruction or their own ill health. Animal welfare just isn't the core argument in a framework if it excuses eating less of some animals. It's broken logic. By reducing animal intake, you are still eating some animals and this is not a compassionate choice. It certainly isn't a vegan approach. Reducetarianism can be a way for some people to transition into living a vegan lifestyle but the message of veganism is clearly not about reducing, but rather removing your dependence on all animals and animal derived products to the best of your ability. A cow that is not being killed for your dinner on Monday will not thank you for being sent to the slaughterhouse later in the week to satisfy your steak craving.

Reducetarianism also leads to speciesism, the phenomenon that permits humans to attach more value to the lives and wellbeing of certain animals at the expense of others. People reducing their animal consumption might choose to eat fish over cows, or chickens over pigs. If someone believes it is acceptable for some animals to die for their food, they need to make a decision about which animals that will involve. The problem with this approach is obviously grounded in our understanding that all animals suffer, so a reducetarian will try and justify to themselves that some animals suffer less than others. Animals might not all contribute equal amounts to the problems of pollution and disease, but they can most definitely all suffer and experience pain, fear and an overwhelming desire to stay alive and unharmed.

Reducing your intake of, and dependence on, animals in your life can be a legitimate way to reach the end goal of veganism and if that is the way that works for you nobody can tell you it's wrong. However, the trend of vegan organisations and activists promoting the 'meat reducer' approach as an ideal is not in the best interest of veganism. As vegans, it is our responsibility to lead by example and trumpet the message that it is an obtainable lifestyle choice. There is no need for us to make allowances or promote baby steps. People do that on their own during their journey to living vegan.

Our vegan message should be unwavering, concise and clear so when an individual is ready to hear it, they get the unfiltered and full-strength version of what living vegan means. It is of course our duty to point people in the direction of the meat replacements and dairy free products that they will use during a transition, but at no point should we be projecting Meat Free Monday as good enough. It's a good start for some people, but veganism isn't a flexible concept and we shouldn't present it as such. There is only one way to end suffering of farmed animals and that is to not kill them for food. A little less killing is still death and suffering, so veganism is the answer; reducing how many animals you eat is not.

Another clear distinction we need to make when promoting the values and concept of veganism is just how fundamentally different it is to vegetarianism.

Veganism and vegetarianism are more often than not lumped together on restaurant menus and by mainstream journalists, but it is our job to explicitly explain the distance between these two lifestyle choices. Eating vegetarian food is looked on as a kinder way to live by many people, but I'm here to tell you that it contributes to animal suffering and death on an immense scale. While vegetarianism is often a launching pad for people to start thinking about going vegan, it is not a kind or compassionate way to live.

Let's unpack this last sentence a little.

If you drink milk from cows because you believe a harmless and benign industry is behind the product, you have to be made aware of a few truths. As we've discussed, cows don't magically produce milk like some sort of non-stop beverage fountains, as some stand-alone miracle of nature. They produce milk because they are responding to being or having been pregnant. The milk that a dairy cow makes is food for the baby her body is expecting to feed.

In a process that is nothing short of horrendous, cows are artificially inseminated and their babies are taken from them immediately following their birth. If the babies were left to bond and hang out with their mothers, those pesky and troublesome youngsters would get their lips on all that cow milk that humans want. So the male calves are taken away to either be raised in cramped, lonely conditions in order to become veal, raised as meat cattle, or killed immediately in order for them to be used as a by-product without incurring the expense of being fed for a few months.

The female calves are mostly used for milk production. As explained above, they enter the cycle of being impregnated, having their children taken immediately after birth, being milked by dangerous and harmful mechanical equipment, and then being impregnated again. In what sounds like nothing short of hell on earth, dairy cows go through this shocking process until they are too sick or frail to be deemed viable. That is when they are killed for cheap meat.

Buying milk products creates a demand that results in a cow being subjected to the repeated experience of being impregnated, living through the trauma of being separated from a child, and rigorous milking that can create painful and harmful lacerations on the udders. Oh yeah, then they experience being killed following a few years of this trauma. Choosing vegetarian products and foods over vegan means you are directly contributing to this process. When we start to unpack where vegetarian food comes from, it becomes clear that it is nowhere near as a compassionate choice as veganism.

Another area in which vegetarianism falls well short of veganism is egg production. As much as a lot of egg producers want us to believe they are supplying a kinder product, this industry is responsible for immeasurable suffering, and vegetarians eating eggs because they think it is a kinder option need to consider some challenging facts. Just like dairy, the cruelty and suffering surrounding eggs is the perfect example of why vegetarianism shouldn't be conflated with veganism.

Egg laying birds are crowded into tiny spaces that are lacking light, clean air and space for the animals to explore their natural instincts and habits. The chickens experience immense physical and psychological distress due to cramped conditions, living in a space equivalent to the size of an A4 piece of paper. They suffer deformities and physical ailments resulting from overcrowding and stress.

Chickens don't just lay a never-ending supply of eggs just for the hell of it. The animals usually produce eggs until their nest is full. They then sit on their eggs in order to incubate them. The process of producing eggs drains a lot of nutrients from a chicken's body, so any eggs that are not fertilised need to be eaten by the bird to ensure it doesn't become frail and ill. Obviously, egg farms are not in the business of allowing chickens to replenish themselves physically this way because that would be eating into profits. Therefore, egg laying hens keep producing eggs to satisfy their natural desire while egg farmers take them away. The process continues until the hens become too drained and their bodies to brittle to continue. Yep, and then they get killed. This leaching of nutrients from the hen's body happens whether they live in a field, in a factory farm, or even if they are your darling rescue birds living blissfully in your backyard coop made with love. You are making them lay more than they naturally would when you take and eat their eggs.

Of course an industry that relies on female birds to continually turn out unfertilised eggs for humans has no place for male chickens. In hatcheries all over the planet, male chicks are separated from the female chicks and killed in various ways. I'm not sure there would be any pleasant way to be killed on a factory farm but the fate of male chicks often minutes after they enter the world seems particularly grotesque. The baby birds are tossed onto a conveyor belt that drops them into a machine that thrashes them into pieces with blades. Other male chicks might find their demise comes about as a result of gassing. Another disposal method is for hundreds of these babies to be bagged up alive and buried or simply left to suffocate.

So a vegetarian lifestyle is actually not a compassionate choice when we consider the suffering of dairy cows, calves, egg hens and their children. Vegan choices being made over vegetarian choices is the only way we can be certain that we are not contributing to this kind of relentless suffering. We need to be clear that while vegetarianism can be a valuable stepping stone for people on a compassionate journey, veganism is the end goal when it comes to challenging brutal and systemic treatment of farmed animals. We shouldn't say veganism and vegetarianism are two sides of the same coin. They are vastly different ideas and only one of these concepts considers animal suffering in a more global sense.

FIRM AND FRIENDLY

To stand up and defend veganism (and its clear and inflexible definition) is not the same as shaming non-vegans. As people living vegan lifestyles, we lead by example while being kind and inclusive to as many humans as we can. Our message isn't one of ridiculing those who are not yet living vegan, but rather an approach of existing in line with our beliefs that animals are not ours to eat, wear and use.

My approach to veganism is about being firm but friendly. We are vegan for a reason and that reason can only be disseminated effectively if we practise what we preach. If someone asks me if eating dairy only once a week is preferable to eating it three times a week, I'll tell them yes, but I'll also add that no dairy at all in a week is the optimum. Every time I'll say that and I'll never shy away from the chance to explain to an interested person that industrialised farming does not give us compassionate consumer options. Of course we can congratulate people on their milestones and the small victories they experience during their transition, but we should never convey the sentiment that reducing is the end goal.

Animals suffer extreme physical, emotional and psychological pain during the processes associated with them being used by humans. As a vegan who has now dedicated my life to reducing this suffering, the promotion of reducing has no place in my campaigning. My message is simple and clear. Vegan means vegan and it is our duty to make people understand why. It doesn't mean reducing animal products. It doesn't mean backyard eggs. It doesn't mean plant-based but still wearing wool and feathers. It doesn't mean honey is an acceptable cheat. It doesn't mean eating cheese on pizza night is cool. It means zero tolerance and that's what I'll tell anyone who asks me. I'll say it in a friendly voice but there is no room for movement in my message.

Veganism is not about weight control and when we hear or see this misconception being promoted, we should challenge it. Take the time to make it known that choosing a vegan lifestyle is more than food choices and it certainly is not a shortcut to a bikini body. This is not for some purist idealism or wanting to seem holier than thou, but rather to help compassionate people come to a deeper understanding of how their individual choices can help improve outcomes for animals and lessen suffering on the planet. Victories for animals come faster and more assuredly when we spread our unwavering message with a kind conviction.

Victories for animals are not won by being apologetic or by trying to gently coax them out of non-vegans. These social situations where we assert our reasons for being vegan might at times feel slightly uncomfortable, but that is a tiny price to pay when you measure it up against the crucial contribution your actions make in the fight for improving outcomes for animals.

Recharge and Refuel

Now I feel it's time to talk about the most obvious vegan food, or at least the most joked about ingredient. Tofu is one of those things non-vegans who haven't grown up with it in their culture never give much thought to, unless they are making a tofu-based joke at the expense of a plant-based eater, but it is also the one food stuff that many of us can't imagine living without once we make the commitment to a vegan lifestyle.

The secret to enjoyable tofu is all about the seasoning, but the secret secret is all about pressing the excess water from a block of tofu before marinating it. I don't know the science behind this marvel, but believe me when I tell you tofu holds onto the flavour so much better if you invest a little time into pressing it beforehand and the texture goes to another level. You can purchase a tofu-pressing contraption or make use of heavy wooden chopping boards and heavy cans already in your kitchen to press the excess liquid from your tofu.

CHAPTER FOUR

ETHICAL VEGAN

> As a vegan, you have a responsibility to not limit your compassion simply to caring about animals. People matter, too.

When we reach a point in our lives where we find ourselves committing to veganism, a lot of us take our foot off the pedal and think we can coast along in our compassion. This isn't unusual. We like to think we are doing the best we can and can easily convince ourselves we are sitting at the pinnacle of kindness, but the truth is most of us can be doing a whole lot more. Remind yourself that most vegans were previously vegetarian and thought THAT was the pinnacle of compassion. Yes, we can always do better.

This chapter is here to remind us that saving animals from suffering isn't the only thoughtful thing in which you should be investing your time, energy and attention. One of my favourite throwaway lines that I love to bandy about is 'people don't need to limit their acts of compassion to just one area of caring'. You can be all about the animals AND want to resist other forms of oppression such as racism, homophobia, sexism, transphobia, wealth disparity, ableism, colonialism and body shaming. And please feel free to resist any other evil forces I've omitted, too.

This might seem daunting to some of you, but it's also an exciting and ultimately rewarding undertaking. As a vegan or future vegan, you have to face up to difficult and unpleasant truths that our society normalises. When you find your motivation to live in the most compassionate way that you can, you have to also find ways to challenge a lot of mainstream thinking. This means you will be in a position where you can extend your compassionate thinking to include the wellbeing of humans, not just non-human animals. You can push yourself to become aware of people-related injustice and suffering and try to combat it through your own behaviour and choices. In this chapter I want to take a look at where this injustice exists in society as a whole, as well as in our vegan communities, and conclude with discussing what we can do about it.

CAPITALISM: THE GLOBAL TOOL OF OPPRESSION

Like pretty much everything we experience or partake in, veganism on a mainstream level is rooted deeply in capitalism, which is powered by Eurocentric (read as white) history, forces and interests. I don't mean to insult your intelligence but of course the individuals who benefit the most from male-dominated Eurocentrism are white men. The system you and I exist within is designed and maintained to benefit very few at the expense of the majority.

Looking at our world through this lens of systemic and organised multiple oppressions is necessary in order for us to understand the part we play and how we can begin to enact change on personal, community and global levels.

The injustices we experience in our world are powered by (amongst other things) racism, colonialism and capitalism. The systems that oppress humans and the systems that exploit animals are all driven by the same inequitable power structures that exist to feed wealth and prosperity back into the ruling elite. Mainstream veganism as we know it today really is just another construct of this system reliant on selling things and hoarding wealth for some of the people on the planet, so it is our responsibility to recognise, resist and dismantle the framework holding it all together as we also push for better outcomes for animals. It is not enough to simply try to not use discriminatory or hurtful language while we eat tofu hot dogs and aquafaba meringue. By exploring our compassion simply with personal food choices, we are only applying a temporary wrapping to the wound of mass animal exploitation unless we ask people to go vegan AND challenge the very power imbalances that make it all possible in the first place.

CHECK YOUR PRIVILEGE

While I am sometimes marginalised and oppressed with regards to my sexuality and weight, I understand that I also live with extreme privilege because I am a white, cis-gendered and able-bodied man. It's the white man part of me that gets a lot of people to listen to the fat and gay parts of me. The modern world is designed to reward me for simply being me at the expense of people who are not me.

We need to know our own place in the world in order to be the most positive force we can be. So, with that in mind, let me start by exploring my understanding of my privilege for a short while before we move on to a plan of action.

I grew up in a poor family with a lot of abuse and sadness in a town where gay kids like me were routinely harassed by law enforcement and local homophobes, but I survived when many people around me didn't. Inequitable systems of oppression were in place to benefit me as a white man even while I was being targeted for my perceived sexuality. People around me who didn't present as white men had safety and opportunity taken away or denied to them.

I left school at age fifteen and moved out of my family home. Even though I didn't complete the most basic high school requirements, I was never out of employment from the moment I left the school gates for the final time. Of course, a lot of that employment was dreadful and underpaid, but the point is that even as an uneducated young person I was employed for any position for which I applied and nobody can tell me my appearance wasn't responsible. I was able to earn a desperately needed income for food and accommodation when a lot of people my age were discriminated against because of institutionalised racism embedded in Australian society.

An adult close to me sexually abused women in my family and these women have lived with the ongoing trauma of that abuse. As a young man, I was statistically less likely to be abused by this person and I wasn't.

My teenage friends and I were searched by the police with alarming regularity during our often drunken nights wandering the streets of our hometown, however, indigenous Australian young people in the same predicament didn't get off with just a warning or even with their lives in a lot of instances. The worst thing to happen to my group of white friends was watching our cheap sparkling wine being poured down the storm water drain while the police laughed at us and ridiculed our clothing. We were not arrested, detained or physically assaulted thanks to our white skin and we were afforded privilege, consideration and relative physical safety during these acts of police surveillance. This was not the case for young people who didn't look like us.

There is a story I think of quite often involving a young man in my hometown. He lived with a physical disability that resulted in him walking with a limp. I would smile at him as he passed by my workplace maybe once a week. We were the same age and we both recognised the other as a queer teenager in a sad town where our kind was not celebrated. We both started going to the same gay bar as teenagers where we mixed with a lot of older people. One terrible night, my hometown comrade was targeted by an older man who took him to a dark alley behind the gay bar and brutally bashed him until he was no longer alive. I found myself in countless compromised situations as a young gay man but I didn't find myself targeted for living with a disability. To understand how people with disabilities are more often targets of violence, search for statistics in your local area and be prepared to be upset by what you find.

Following on from decades of dead end jobs, I secured a place at university to follow up on my interest and desire to become a schoolteacher. The four-year undergraduate degree culminated with a multi-month practical placement in a real classroom. I was the only person out of my group of friends offered a job by the school at the end of the practical teaching placement. I was also the only one of said group who was identifiable as a white man and I'm comfortable in saying that I was nowhere close to being the most accomplished or hard-working student teacher amongst my cohort.

I'm not reflecting on these memories to get a pat on the back for being progressively aware, I'm telling you because it is crucial for those of us living with and benefitting from privilege to understand that the animal rights movement is not separate to everything I've described above. I have discovered that if I want to be a worthy activist for animals I must also learn to resist and challenge oppression in multiple forms within vegan circles. Vegan businesses, vegan activist groups, vegan socials and vegan online spaces all operate within the same systemic framework of oppression that favours me in the ways I described above. If I am being rewarded, someone is being oppressed. That is how it works.

COMPLEX SOCIETY: COMPLEX PROBLEMS

The vegan movement is part of modern society, and so all these issues affect us too. Broader mainstream society is dripping with opportunities to oppress people while hearing the voices of and promoting the interests of the rich and the white. It's a tolerated and bizarrely celebrated part of modern society. It stands to reason that as veganism moves more to being an accepted niche within mainstream life, the more we will see capitalistic forces that favour very few being employed in the promotion of the vegan lifestyle as well as all associated marketing related to selling the vegan package to as many people as possible.

With a little planning and a desire to do better, we can begin to exercise our responsibility for addressing the multiple oppressions affecting us, and the people around us, as we go through life as vegans dedicated to improving outcomes for animals. We can struggle to dismantle and change the system at the same time as working to protect and promote those of us living within it.

Since I have identified as a fat person for a lot of my adult life, let's start with the rampant problem of body and fat shaming within the vegan community. Vegan food companies, animal activist groups and mainstream media representations of veganism, as well as individual humans, all work together to perpetuate unrealistic and damaging standards of body size and appearance. In simpler terms, we are sold products using imagery that makes us feel bad about who we are and that we aren't the finest example of a human being.

People for the Ethical Treatment of Animals (PETA) is notorious for their divisive advertising campaigns using body shaming tactics to try and entice non-vegans to switch to an animal free lifestyle or diet. The organisation has routinely used images of fat people alongside derogatory or inflammatory statements linking weight to laziness, ignorance and having an undesirable and sexless body.

Being fat is a lot more complex than being ignorant. People can be fat for various reasons including genetic makeup, injury, long-term illness, depression, financial constraints, access to nutritious food, age, abuse, neglect, inadequate healthcare – and the list can go on and on. There is not one simple reason why anyone is fat and to suggest that it is simply because they don't eat vegan food is wrong, insulting and hurtful. I'm not putting this out there for consideration, I'm stating it as fact. I live through this very real situation.

LaURa BeCK is a writer living in Los Angles, the founder of superstar vegan blog Vegansaurus, and one of the most compassionate people on the planet. We often cruise around town when I am visiting; eating vegan froyo and talking about our dreams to star in a reality television show together about fat vegan bloggers.

'Vegans can sometimes use body shaming as a tactic to introduce people to veganism and it's the opposite of the compassion that is meant to be at the centre of the movement. Veganism is not a weight loss scheme. It's a lifestyle that values compassion at its core.

'When we tell people they'll lose weight when they become vegan, not only is that a lie (I gained weight because I started caring more about food than ever before) but it also makes people think they're "doing veganism wrong" when they don't lose weight. For some people, this line of thinking encourages the use of veganism as a crutch for disordered eating. Not only is that harmful to the person, it's harmful to veganism because those

> people will never stay vegan. Diets don't work, and that includes veganism. But lifestyle changes often do work. I connect on a core level to the "do the least amount of harm possible" aspect of veganism and that includes having compassion for animals and people, including the fact that we're all different shapes and sizes – and that's awesome!'

People mostly understand why they are fat. When strangers offer me 'expert' advice such as cutting down on sugar while upping my exercise regime from nothing to something, I have to politely inform them that I understand how the science of the human body works. I also feel the need to let them know my body is none of their business. Just as I do not welcome comments on my size and shape, I urge everyone reading to see the act of shaming non-vegans about their body size as unhelpful for our cause and damaging to humans. It is not our business to make personal observations and critiques of other people's bodies. To do so is as far away from compassion as you can possibly get and it is in fact an undeniable act of oppression.

Another important exercise in flexing your compassion has to do with respecting language that doesn't belong to you or to veganism.

One sure fire way to NOT be the kindest and most compassionate vegan you can is to appropriate the language and imagery of oppressive struggles as a way to draw attention to the animal rights movement. Many activists find themselves comparing industrialised farming to slavery or the Holocaust. It is alluring to reach for something so undeniable in its horror, renown and infamy to conjure emotion and grab attention but what you are also doing is minimising the reality of what people went through and are still living through today.

Industrialised farming has enough of its own atrocities that can be explained in clear language attributable to that distinct situation. There is no need to use language that does not belong to the vegan movement. Historical and current references related to slavery, genocide and sexual violence against humans are not ours to use as we please. It is harmful and disrespectful to do so.

I could fill many chapters on just racism within vegan circles alone. If you are of the mind that racism isn't a problem with vegan communities then you might be one of these people who believe racism isn't a problem in general. There are plenty of people who you should investigate the views of if you are interested in resisting racism and transforming the way you contribute.

Just as it is outside of vegan circles, racism manifests in countless ways within vegan movements and communities.

We see fewer opportunities for non-white vegan business owners, less press and media for non-white vegan personalities, racist and colonial power imbalances in full force, limitations imposed around who gets to speak and be heard, invisibilisation and exoticisation of non-white veganism, framing of veganism as a Whole Foods Market side business designed for white people, lack of understanding of how and why non-white vegans organise and socialise on their own terms, and the obsession with celebrities who are more mainstream press friendly (i.e. usually cis-gendered and white in appearance). Mainstream media wants to get in on the ground floor when it comes to the commodification of veganism and they fall right back into their tired and oppressive tricks of focussing on white people when reporting, writing personal profile features and employing clickbait tactics.

Racism in veganism is never clearer than in public awareness campaigns targeting minority or specific ethnic and religious groups. You'll have seen and maybe even participated in campaigns working to shut down Halal abattoirs, end the Yulin festival where eating dog meat is a feature, and, of course, one of the longest-running racially-charged animal rights campaigns going back decades, to dismantle the Japanese whaling industry.

My friend **GEORGE LIN** is somebody who has been extremely vocal about this type of racist vegan campaigning, so I reached out to him to see if he would like to share his thoughts. George is a queer animal rights and social justice activist, vegan food and travel microblogger, and a general loud mouth (his words, not mine!) against all forms of oppression. He is sought out as a vegan food competition judge; is an editor at large for one of the largest vegan publications and a social media influencer for vegan festivals. I would also like to add that George is a really good dancer.

'Asian people who grow up in the West are constantly subjected to racist attacks that manifest themselves in many different forms. One of them is related to the incorrect notion that we all eat "weird" foods that include dogs and cats. This creates a form of "othering" us into some sort of different species that is "exotic" and seen as below the level of Westerners. We are exposed to this form of racism as children and it seriously affects us and our identities. I personally couldn't eat my lunches in school. Lunches that were meticulously prepared by my mom who would wake up at 5 am every day to cook incredibly delicious Taiwanese meals, but I couldn't enjoy them because I didn't want to endure the mocking from other children and even teachers.

'As a vegan adult, I instantly recall those painful childhood moments whenever I see vegans carelessly campaigning against Yulin. Targeting this one festival while so many other forms of animal slaughter are happening in Western nations fuels this "othering" of Asian people. I have seen these animal rights crusaders describe Asian people as barbaric while completely ignoring the fact that cows, pigs and chickens go through the same cruel abuse, that there is an incredibly large amount of Asian animal rights activists tirelessly working to stop the dog meat trade as well as any other forms of animal abuse, plus the overlooked statistic that Asian people compose the largest number of vegetarians and vegans worldwide.

'The speciesism and racism of targeting this festival and not others is blatant. It manipulates the minds of people into believing that dogs are more important than any other species and that Asian people are the sole contributors to dog abuse, ignoring the abuse that many dogs are subjected to in non-Asian societies such as dog fighting rings, puppy mills and instances of dog eating in other regions in the West. In order to move forward,

> vegans need to have a greater understanding of
> social and racial construct. This is not about putting
> humans before animals or the other way around.
> It's ensuring that we are all on the same level. We
> can't ignore any human oppression in our activism,
> because at the end of the day, we need other
> humans to go vegan and be activists. A greater
> comprehension of how our actions can impact
> people with different backgrounds to our own will
> aid in the effectiveness of our activism.'

I couldn't list the ways in which mainstream veganism objectifies women and powers sexism and misogyny. Men dominate speaking panels, women are expected to silently organise, and veganism is sold particularly to women as a weight or body modification tool in order for them to live up to unrealistic physical expectations.

The plight of women who are sexual assault and abuse survivors is appropriated to inject emotion into the animal rights struggle by equating forced insemination of dairy cows with human rape. Women's bodies are used as props to both grab attention for campaigns and titillate consumers into buying plant-based food and clothing.

Basically, we vegans do to women what the rest of the world is doing to them but we dress it up as compassion.

Ableism within the vegan community isn't always as obvious as people using oppressive language and slurs, although of course you should be all over any situation like that or look for support if you need it when challenging people. As allies of people with disabilities we should be addressing lack of representation and visibility in what is advertised to us and the events we attend and host. People with disabilities are rarely asked to participate in panel discussions or consulted for perspectives on vegan campaigning, meaning their life experiences and opinions go unvalued and unnoticed.

Some vegan campaigners will also denigrate non-vegans living with illness as if they are responsible for their situation for not living completely plant-based. I've seen this first-hand when a vegan man publicly shamed a celebrity who had been diagnosed with breast cancer. This man's take away was not in any way compassionate, instead he used his platform to suggest the celebrity would not be in the situation if she had cared about animals and stopped consuming them. In how many ways can we agree that is horrific?

Toxic masculinity is a buzz term thrown around a lot but you had better believe it is ripe and rampant amongst vegans and activist circles. This culture of hypermasculinity erodes social cohesion by promoting the dominant view that to be seen as masculine is the most desirable trait in a human. An approach like this leads to the ridiculing of LGBTQ+ people and women. Vegan advertising and representations of vegan men in the media collude to perpetuate this damaging approach by championing 'tough' athletes, using sexist and misogynistic language to demean men who do not conform to ideals of masculinity, and even making suggestions that you are less of a man if you are unable to please women sexually.

It all comes together in a 'toxic' cocktail of oppression that harms all society including cis-gendered men who identify as straight.

iS YOUR FOOD REALLY CRUELTY-FREE?

Food injustice, food security and farm workers' rights are all topics every vegan should prioritise. Millions of people around the planet are working in exploitative conditions to get kale and carrots to your vegan table. People in your own city and town do not have access to affordable fresh fruit and vegetables. Your vegan lifestyle is not a compassionate choice if workers are being denied fair wages and conditions, children are forced into dangerous situations for harvesting or production, or if you are one of the few people around the world who can afford to make whatever choice you want when it comes to your food

purchases but you don't give thought or consideration to
how it gets onto your plate.

> SaRaH BeNTLeY became vegetarian as a self-
> described precocious nine-year-old and transitioned
> to veganism at age twenty. She says, 'The transition
> happened after a life changing visit to Jamaica as a
> young journalist to write a piece about reggae and I
> found I fell in love with Rastafarian ital food and the
> whole philosophy around it.'
>
> After much soul searching and journeying
> Sarah left journalism to become an organic food
> grower, community gardener and, in 2012, founded
> pioneering charity Made in Hackney (MIH). MIH is
> the UK's only one hundred per cent plant-based
> eco-community kitchen and cookery school. The
> charity offers free and pay-by-donation food growing
> and cooking classes to groups in need, in addition
> to having classes open to all. Sarah describes the
> MIH family as 'a small but hugely dedicated team of
> staff and an amazing army of passionate volunteers
> taking their local, seasonal, organic, plant-based food
> message out into the community.'
>
> 'In my humble opinion, growing your own food
> and cooking local, organic, seasonal, one hundred

per cent plant-based food is a really excellent way of sticking two fingers up to "the man" without having to D-lock yourself to a digger at a fracking site or superglue yourself to a politician. Those types of actions are obviously awesome but we're not all cut out for such hard-core activism. By choosing to eat like this to the best of our abilities and means while co-running an organisation that promotes these choices, we are addressing so many crucial issues at once.

'Food sovereignty, food access, climate change, health of farm workers, health of people, corporate control over our food system, ethical treatment of animals, biodiversity ... it's big. Being vegan – or plant-based – is just the tip of the iceberg. It's a starting point but if you want to consider the whole picture you need to bolt on local (or at least never air freighted), seasonal and organic as much as possible.

'This type of diet is often perceived as the exclusive prevail of yuppies and hipsters, only economically possible for people earning good money or those with a lot of skills in the kitchen and garden. At MIH we choose to focus a lot of our time working with groups who stand to gain the most. That might include people on low incomes, those living with long-term health challenges, vulnerable young people and marginalised communities. We work hard to normalise this type of eating and show people ways it can be accessible while still having loads of fun eating heaps of delicious food.

'It's these groups that suffer disproportionately from health inequalities and lifestyle-induced diseases such as diabetes, obesity, heart disease and certain types of cancers. They're also the groups most likely to be living in food deserts, to be working multiple jobs including shift work, and to be living in areas with high pollution and lower living standards. In terms of health and wellbeing the scales are tipped massively to the negative for them. It's well and good choosing to drink more green smoothies and ditching cows' milk for hemp or whatever but if this way of eating is completely off limits or seemingly inaccessible to huge swathes of our communities then what sort of progress is this?

'We need to bring everyone up together and to think about supportive ways of doing this and extend as much love to our fellow humans as we do to the animals we want to save from the slaughterhouse. That's what we try and do at MIH.'

If we really want to make a difference for humans as well as animals, we need to listen to what the frontline support groups are telling us and take action. There are very real, everyday situations in which you will find yourself where you can make conscious decisions about caring for other humans through your food and lifestyle choices. Organisations such as Made in Hackney and Food Empowerment Project work tirelessly to not only support people who are vulnerable to exploitation, but to also speak to those of us powering inequitable industries through our consumer choices.

> **LAUREN ORNELAS** is Food Empowerment Project's founder and serves as the group's executive director. lauren has been active in the animal rights movement for more than thirty years. She is the former executive director of Viva!USA, a national non-profit vegan advocacy organisation that Viva!UK asked her to start in 1999. While lauren was the director of Viva!USA, she investigated factory farms and ran consumer campaigns. In cooperation with activists across the country, she persuaded US supermarket Trader Joe's to stop selling all duck meat and achieved corporate changes within Whole Foods Market, Pier 1 Imports and others, and she helped

halt the construction of an industrial dairy operation in California. lauren was also the spark that got the founder of Whole Foods Market to become a vegan.

'I went vegan because I didn't want to inflict pain or suffering on other beings. And for those of us who feel this way, it is hard to accept that our food choices could still be contributing to the pain and suffering of others. Unfortunately, just because a food is vegan does not necessarily mean it is cruelty-free. Farm workers who pick produce are treated with grave injustice, from their living conditions to where they work. They work long hours, without adequate pay; women are regularly sexually harassed; and others are exposed to agricultural chemicals. Many women who enter the US from the southern border take birth control pills before they leave home because sexual assault is prevalent en route. Intimidation means many do not speak out about the abuses they face, including wage theft. They sacrifice so that their families can thrive, but barriers are created preventing them from succeeding. Of course, some do beat the odds.

'But it is not just the fruits and vegetables we eat; commodity products such as coffee and chocolate are rife with abuses. In western Africa, child labour and even slavery are widely prevalent in the chocolate industry. I feel it is really important for vegans to be honest about this and do their best to be consistent in their own ethics. No one is perfect, but if compassion or a sense of justice is why someone went vegan, it is important to do our best to do the least harm.

'I believe that the food system has been created by the concept of dominance. Just like non-human animals are treated as if their only purpose is for human consumption. Their bodies have been bizarrely and horrifically transformed into what suits a system that treats them as unfeeling beings, from cutting off their toes and tails to killing them when they are no longer seen as productive. This is a system that has also sought to pretend these are unfeeling beings who would not show emotion when their babies are stolen from them or experience boredom without freedom.

'Human animals in the food system are also treated as mere commodities. They too are seen as beings who are there to serve a purpose. Many Mexicans (who pick produce in the US) are somehow seen as "good workers" or "stronger" than most, when in reality they get hot and exhausted. But they do the work that many others don't want to do because of the lives they want their children to lead. Oppression is currently worked into the economics of food. We do not eat with our ethics and so we devalue the lives of others for cheap food.

'When it comes to addressing the disparity on lack of access to healthy foods in indigenous communities, communities of colour and low-income communities, it will vary on where in the world this is taking place; however, it is important for vegans to admit that it is not easy for every individual to go vegan – it really depends on their financial situation and location. It is extremely important for them to accept that not everyone has or has had the privileges that they might have.

'In most circumstances, if vegans want to contribute to solutions in this area, they can support living wage efforts to make it easier for people to afford healthy foods, financially support community organisations working on these issues, and also speak out against the oppression of people colour and indigenous peoples.

'It would be good for vegans to be involved in or recognise efforts to improve the conditions that workers face by supporting campaigns, boycotts, and other actions called by the workers themselves.

> 'Actually, it is imperative that we do! For all of these issues, we must use our individual choices as well as our collective voices. We must speak out not only against corporations that abuse human and non-humans alike but also unjust legislation and politicians. And we need to use all of the tools we have in the tool box while speaking out against these injustices in all activist forms.'

An important lesson I've learned during my years of interacting with various vegan communities and individuals is the importance of working on understanding my privilege and how it shapes my attitudes surrounding vegan outreach. Knowing how my appearance affords me privilege, which in turn leads to more opportunities for financial security, helps me to consider changing the language I use when asking people to consider making vegan changes in their lives.

I can afford to make choices that other people would view as luxurious or completely unattainable and I have to remind myself that promoting and singing the praises of vegan consumerism can work as an act of oppression. There are many more people on the planet who cannot afford vegan vacations, food ingredients, clothing and personal care products than those who do have the financial means.

Not every person looking at exploring veganism as a lifestyle choice views my spending habits the way I do.

A friend of mine in Mexico was explaining his shoe dilemma to me recently. His work requires him to wear dress shoes for certain functions and he cannot afford or access affordable vegan footwear in his region and shipping shoes in from outside Mexico is not an expense he can accommodate. As his belief in living a vegan lifestyle expands, he is finding himself at odds with certain situations. The best course of action I feel I can take is to support him as a friend in the decisions he has to make and celebrate him for his commitment to compassion while he makes do with the inexpensive vinyl shoes he finds at his nearest discount footwear shop.

ALL FEELS a BiT iNTENSE? TaKE aCTiON!

As you are reading my book, I gather you don't mind me running through a list of 'better practices' when it comes to being a more ethical vegan, in order to add to the insights given by the people I spoke to in this chapter. Speak up if you do mind. Just kidding, I wrote this ages ago and I'm probably sitting in a bar somewhere asking the bartender to tell me what is vegan on tap. So let's recap the chapter with a few basic suggestions for better practice when it comes to being an ethical vegan.

A vegan market I help curate in London has employed a policy to challenge privilege when selecting traders. We give preference to traders who identify as a person with a disability, a member of the LGBTQ+ community, black or minority ethnic (BME) and/or as women. The organisers and I hold the belief that people from these groups in our society are often marginalised due to the privilege afforded people who are straight white cis-gendered men. This is our small way of trying to redress the imbalance in order to help real individuals earn a living outside of an oppressive, competitive and inequitable landscape. There is not one participating business at time of writing this that is exclusively owned or operated by a straight white man. Before you get stressed out and worry about the straight white men who want to cook for a living, believe me when I say there are hundreds of street food markets in that part of the UK that are absolutely overflowing with opportunities for them. They are doing OK from a representational standpoint.

If you're holding an event, there aren't a lot of convincing reasons why you would do so in a location where there are no accessible toilets or only limited access entrances/exits. Lack of suitable access for all guests is oppressive. If you attend an event without access, make it your business to ask the organisers why they weren't able to accommodate guests with access needs. It doesn't matter if the building having access makes your life easier or not, it is simply a way of extending your compassion to be inclusive of people living with disability or those with access requirements.

If you find yourself involved with organising any kind of vegan event, consider employing an inclusive policy to ensure people who are traditionally excluded from vegan spaces are given preference. You never have to look very hard to find a white vegan to speak on a panel but always turning to the usual suspects is not inclusive or equitable. Look for presenters and speakers who will give a broader representation of what being vegan means. Be sure to have a policy of inviting LGBTQ+ vegans, women, women of colour, vegans of colour, and people living with disabilities to be part of organising committees and to be voices addressing mainstream vegan events.

Of course, all of these examples of best behaviour can be applied in other areas of your life and not just when you are being a super vegan. Who is often left out and how can they be included? Are there any barriers stopping people from varying backgrounds from contributing equally and what can you do about them? Consider inclusivity at work functions, social gatherings, on sports teams, even family gatherings and any group activity in which you are involved.

Use non-gendered language whenever appropriate or when you are just not certain of how someone identifies. It takes nothing away from your general happiness but the power of not mis-gendering another human is a fundamentally powerful tool. Why not put it to good use all the time?

Don't appropriate language that has historically described the suffering or death of an oppressed group in order to add drama to your animal rights campaigning. Be active in reminding the vegans around you of how this erases, minimalises and denigrates survivors of historic and current abuse and acts of oppression.

Don't sexualise food. This is one of the simplest ways to be an inclusive and thoughtful vegan. Apart from there being zero reasons to call a donut sexy or label your dinner as #veganfoodporn, this use of language can actually work to perpetuate systems of oppressions that marginalise and objectify women. I know this is a tough topic to get on board with because we are so very used to every aspect of our lives being repackaged to us in sexy ad speak. But take a moment to think of exactly what messages are being transmitted when food is framed within the language of hyper sexualisation or fetishisation. There are clear similarities between the salacious language used to describe sexual fantasies surrounding women and the phenomenon of sexualising meat. It is sometimes difficult to know what is being described by the use of words such as juicy, plump, succulent and naughty and this is clearly the point of food advertisers. There are countless ways in which you can celebrate your love of food publicly without relying on these tired and unhelpful phrases.

Donate time, skills or money to organisations that are actively working to redress food injustice. If you have enough money to care for you and your loved ones without too much stress, you probably have enough disposable time or money to help support the crucial work of groups such as Food Empowerment Project and Made in Hackney. Capitalism doesn't allow all of us to be rich or even comfortable, so please consider what you can do to redistribute wealth and challenge food insecurity through your own personal choices.

A powerful way to resist animal exploitation and the oppressive forces of capitalism is to start a vegan workers' cooperative or join an existing one in your town or city. Whether it is a shared ownership café or a grocery cooperative, these collaborative spaces keep profits out of the hands of multinational corporations and in the pockets of the local community. Customers learn about veganism in a positive and affirming way from a business that has human and animal interests at the core of its philosophy.

Black Cat Café in London, UK, is the perfect example of what a collaborative and shared business can do for its community while at the same time promoting veganism. They support local chefs with free or discounted kitchen hire, serve nutritious vegan meals at extremely reasonable prices and make group decisions giving each member of the cooperative equal say regardless of personal situations or realities that might otherwise put them at a disadvantage in another work environment.

Recognise your own privilege and consider how much power it affords you. Be aware of it and don't always take what is offered or available, whether that is space to speak or actual physical space. Be mindful that your privilege and all it affords you is not only inequitable, it also works as a form of oppression in its own way.

Elevate minority voices. Look to see if people who are most-often marginalised and silenced are being called on to speak or are in organising roles. If you have the opportunity to ask the opinion of someone living with oppression, listen carefully and magnify what they have to say. Be sure to share insights and opinions about multiple oppressions without erasing the voices of the people who are living those very lives. Use your own story and the stories of others to explain how a vegan can work at being a better person who doesn't only concern themselves with improving outcomes for animals.

If you feel safe and able to do so, call out people who are using oppressive language at vegan and non-vegan events. Ask a friend or someone willing to help you if you do not feel safe. People sometimes do not understand how their language and actions can make those around them feel threatened, excluded or targeted. If you are a white vegan, make it your responsibility to help educate other white vegans about racism, privilege and colonial attitudes. If you identify as a man, tell other men how their language and actions can make women feel unsafe in vegan spaces. Call people out for ableist, transphobic and body shaming language and take the time to explain how it affects people if they genuinely don't understand how words oppress. We have a responsibility to keep other vegans and non-vegans (yes, they are people with delicate feelings too) safe from harm and oppression. It is not the sole responsibility of the oppressed to speak out against the oppressor, rather it is the job of all of us to stand up together. Be considerate and find ways to challenge these behaviours when possible.

Become an expert letter and email writing champion in order to tell vegan food companies that oppressive language and images have no place in advertising to our community. Use social media to make them aware of the fact that you do not appreciate or accept the use of sexism, body shaming, toxic masculinity and white exceptionalism as tools to sell veganism as a concept or vegan products to the world. It perpetuates harmful forces that make people feel bad about who they are while cementing long entrenched power imbalances that favour very few.

Support charities and activist groups that do not rely on sexism, racism, misogyny, body shaming and homophobia to sell veganism. As discussed earlier in this chapter, PETA often relies on shock advertising tactics at the expense of real humans. If you have money or time to offer a charity, search around for organisations that do not participate in using violence and oppressive acts to garner attention to help spread the vegan message. Question anyone who asks you if vegan men can still be tough and sexy by turning it back into a discussion of toxic masculinity. We don't need to accept this dominant discourse that is damaging all of us, especially those of us already at risk.

Don't use oppressive language traditionally employed to denigrate people with disabilities and mental health challenges in your fight to promote veganism. This might come across as slightly trite when first being confronted with this idea, but look for more inclusive language when attempting to describe your intentions and thoughts. Factory farming isn't crazy or mental. It is an upsetting systemic form of suffering and death. Consider where your first choice of language originates and always push yourself to do better each time.

As a way of wrapping up this weighty chapter, I turned to an online acquaintance and ally to succinctly round up this idea of living as an ethical vegan.

Michele Kaplan is a self-described geeky intersectional activist, vegan and proudly disabled artist and writer who gets around via her motorised wheelchair named Lulabelle. She is the host of Rebelwheels NYC, an intersectional disability themed YouTube show, and is the creator/administrator of the What Is Ableism project.

Michele stated to me, 'Veganism is doing the least harm and the most good for the earth and the animals. When vegans knowingly and unapologetically engage in oppressive behaviour such as racism, sexism, ableism, Islamophobia, sizeism, homophobia and more, it makes any vegan movement less welcoming. Less welcoming equals less allies, which only hurts the earth and animals. Because of this, one could reasonably argue that engaging in such behaviour is not vegan.'

RECHARGE AND REFUEL

There is nothing I love more than battered and fried food. Give me crunchy textures and savoury flavours any day of the week and I'm happy. One of the true champions of the vegan food scene is battered cauliflower. It's simple to make, extremely versatile and can be used in everything from tacos to stir-fry.

Here's a simple recipe for vegan batter. Once you've got the hang of it, you could switch things up a little by adding hot sauce, chilli, garlic or mustard powder to the batter, or get busy learning the tricks of beer battered frying.

Mix together 125g/4½ oz/1 cup flour with 1 tablespoon of cornflour/cornstarch, half a teaspoon of baking powder, a pinch of salt and any other flavourings you want to try out. Slowly pour in 240ml/9fl oz/1 cup ice cold water while whisking, and mix until smooth.

Dust each piece of whatever you're battering with additional flour, then dip it into the batter to coat well. Drop into a pan of hot oil and fry until golden.

My top tip for consuming? Liberally squeeze lime juice all over your crunchy bite-sized cauliflower for the ultimate finger food. Perfect for parties with all your buddies or even a party of one. You deserve it!

Chapter Five

THE IMPORTANCE OF COMMUNITY

> Effective, united and empowered communities work to improve outcomes for their own members as well as contributing to wellness and equitable outcomes on a global scale.

A lot of my personal energy over the past six or seven years has gone into trying to create spaces for vegans to be vegan.

The world isn't always the most accepting place when it comes to individuals opting out of something as socialised and celebrated as eating, wearing and using animals, and, as such, we often need some time away from the dominant culture to gather our thoughts. The seismic shift veganism creates in your world can leave you feeling isolated and without peers, especially when the people you love and surround yourself with are not on the same page. When we need time apart from non-likeminded people, we don't always want that time to be spent alone.

It was mostly my own emotional needs as a vegan that pushed me into creating events and spaces in which plant-based approaches were the norm. I needed a little company as I was not feeling surrounded by a lot of likeminded people. Let me give you a small insight into the how and the why.

My partner Josh and I left the world of red-bellied snakes and weekends spent swimming in the surf in order to move to the UK in 2010. I had recently graduated with a teaching degree and I was keen to put my theory into practice by educating young people. We boarded the seemingly endless flight from Brisbane, Australia to London with big ideas and unknown possibilities jostling for attention in our heads. Josh was returning home to England after nine years living in Australia and I was simply excited for a new adventure following on from four years of full time study.

Upon touching down in London, we spent a few weeks visiting friends and family before I threw myself into a teaching job in the north of the country. The shock of ankle deep snow and travelling to and from work in the dark was second only to the complete and utter horror of not being able to understand what any of the children were saying at the Yorkshire school where I crash landed.

I lasted a few months in the Yorkshire wilderness (actually the busy market town of Halifax, but you understand I'm going for drama here) and it wasn't completely the fault of the children when I decided I had to get out. The vegan part of me was desperate for some interaction with likeminded souls and I truly thought London would be the place for dynamic, life-altering vegan experiences. I was tired of baked potatoes with hummus being one of my only options at cafés (this is not made up for dramatic effect) and it was time for me to hit out and find the promised land of seitan cutlets and vegan cupcakes.

At this point, I was desperate for validation of my lifestyle choice on a grand scale. I wanted parties, I wanted vegan choices, and I desperately wanted people to tell me I was on the right track. Of course, I can't pretend that London wasn't a few steps up the plant-based ladder on my arrival when compared with where I had just been, but even still I struggled to find exciting and interesting social events where I would be able to feel celebrated in my veganism.

Josh and I had once attended a vegan potluck dinner in California that had inspired me to think I could transfer the idea to London. Not the part where the Californian vegans made me stand in a circle and announce what I was grateful for before I was permitted to eat anything, but the wonderful concept of strangers and acquaintances coming together to share homemade food in a friendly, inclusive and relaxed setting.

There was something so touching yet simple about being a part of a shared experience focussed on food. I felt as though people were willing to drop a few layers of defences because we had all committed to coming together in a non-threatening situation where we had already heavily considered each other's feelings. I put in a lot of effort to my food offering because I wanted to impress the other attendees, I wanted them to get along with me, and I wanted them to be happy.

And so, newly settled in London, I created London Vegan Potluck. I wanted to create a space where compassionate people would be guaranteed at least one night a month where their decision to explore their commitment to eating vegan would not be ridiculed or questioned. It might sound a little difficult to believe but ribbing and harassment can be a daily occurrence for a lot of vegans and London Vegan Potluck would be a break from all of that type of annoyance.

Locating a space in central London that would allow outsiders to bring their own food wasn't an easy task, but the fabulous Mellissa Morgan of legendary vegan bakery Ms Cupcake put in a lot of effort to arrange space for my event in the arcade outside her Brixton shop front once a month. Our approach, particularly in those early months, was very DIY, but we quickly realised that it was working, and that people were coming together with a common goal. It was a wonderful time of getting to know other vegans, exploring new foods and being part of what would turn into an unstoppable social scene for vegan Londoners.

As the size of the crowd we were welcoming grew, we moved locations so we could fit more people in. Over the four full years London Vegan Potluck ran, we welcomed guests from the USA, Europe and Australia and participant numbers often passed one hundred hungry people. I recall several occasions when potluck fanatics would swing by on their way to the airport with a homemade dish because they couldn't fathom the idea of missing one single month.

Running the potluck was tiring work for me and Josh. I lost track of how many chairs I stacked, how many dishes I scrubbed, and how much red wine I mopped up from the floor with paper towels. However, the heart-warming reaction and genuine appreciation we received from the overwhelmingly positive attendees made the troubles drift away. We found that people loved the opportunity to meet other vegans, to share recipes, to challenge themselves to cook things they wouldn't usually, and to really feel part of something.

My friend ▮▮▮▮ had been a vegetarian since birth, and comes from a family background where no one eats meat. She was an early attendee at London Vegan Potluck, so I asked her how she came to attend Potluck, and how being part of the community around the night affected her.

'To begin with, I didn't know any other vegans. I wanted some advice on where they ate out, what their favourite meals were and of course I wanted their opinions on the top cheese substitutes! I'd heard about Meetup.com so I went online, wrote a profile and was delighted to find a lot of vegan events happening in my beloved home city of London. London Vegan Potluck stood out instantly. Cooking and sharing what I'd made with lots of people is so far up my street. I come from a large family where a big part of gatherings and festivals revolves around food. I was even more delighted to find that the event took place on a weekday evening in central London, not far from where I work.

'I can't remember what I made for my first London Vegan Potluck but I remember the absolutely wonderful feeling I experienced during that event. I wasn't alone! Everyone was so friendly, so welcoming and kind. There were lots of delicious, colourful things to try and people said nice things about what I'd brought along to share.

'From that point on and for the next three years, the Potluck was a set date in my diary. Barring trips abroad, I didn't miss a single one and I have so many happy memories of those events. I made some fantastic friends who I still have in my life to this day and hopefully for many more years to come. I learned about lots of different types of cuisine and found some great new ideas. It gave me the chance to make big or challenging items that I'd always wanted to make, but that I wouldn't have made if it was just for me. I absolutely loved it.'

It wasn't just a place for Mirel to explore her culinary skills and make new friends. London Vegan Potluck also became a valuable space in which Mirel and her family could share experiences.

> 'A year or so after I first started attending, I convinced my parents to come and join me. They weren't sure what to expect the first time but duly cooked some dishes and turned up at the venue on the correct Wednesday evening. It wasn't long before they decided they loved it too and they became regulars. It was lovely to be known as a family of attendees, because to my knowledge we were the only family group who did this and it was a special experience to share together. The Potluck had a unique, positive atmosphere and was always something we looked forward to on a monthly basis.'

However, despite the runaway success of London Vegan Potluck, there was one aspect of it that occasionally played on my mind. There is an overwhelming emphasis on the culinary component of veganism, whereas in reality there aren't many of us that would consider ourselves Michelin starred chefs. The positive side of the Potluck was that it was very down to earth and it was often the homemade, no frills food that got the most positive reaction. And yet there was a genuine fear for some people when it came to having to watch other attendees eat and possibly judge their culinary achievements. Imagine being in a room with one hundred vegans who were all extremely vocal about their food opinions. I can understand how the situation wasn't for everyone!

So I was inspired to create a companion event that would allow for vegans and vegan-curious people to socialise without the stress of being required to cook a homemade dish.

The idea to create a monthly space solely for the purpose of vegan socialising was prompted by a discussion I had with Jason Das, one of the founders of the Vegan Drinks events in New York City. Jason put it to me there was no good reason why this event wasn't already taking place in a city the size of London. It was exactly the kick I needed to get it off the ground in the UK capital.

London Vegan Drinks became the home away from home for a lot of people who didn't want to cook for strangers. Our group of vegans and vegan-friendly revellers would converge on a central London spot one night each month to get to know each other, lend support and generally just enjoy being part of something. A community.

WHO BENEFITS FROM VEGAN EVENTS?

So that's the story of how I came to set up my own events that became a gathering point for the vegan community, and eventually turned into little communities of their own. They became very valued by people who had made the big leap into a way of life that can be different to how most other people live, and attracted those who wanted to meet others with similar experiences and outlooks. They had the power to engage people, and to make them feel valued and celebrated for being vegan as well as for being who they were outside of veganism.

London Vegan Potluck and London Vegan Drinks also empowered those who attended to determine what sort of events they wanted to see in the future. They were inspired to go away and create their own thing. So many wonderful events sprung forth from these foundations, and similar social nights can now be found around the UK and mainland Europe, started by people who were once valuable members of those early London meetings. Friendships were forged that are still going strong today and just last week I received my first vegan wedding invitation from people who met at London Vegan Drinks. Stay happy, Roisin and Ben!

The events are the first piece of the puzzle. They are safe opportunities and spaces in which people can interact, explore and develop their kind approach to life, as well as start to collaborate on personal and community levels with others. Veganism might be the thing that brings a lot of people together, but so much more can spring forth from these social events.

Because the events were built to consider differing realities and experiences, members of this community were happy to listen to and raise up minority voices. This in turn encouraged members to take charge on future community events, which catered to various streams and niches within our vegan community. The launch and success of Queer Vegan Disco, a monthly low cost dance party for LGBTQ+ people and their friends, for example, was testament to this theory of people going to existing events and then determining what they want or need. The rush of events that flourished from these first initial gatherings is testament to how vegans wanted and needed to socialise and gather on their terms.

Vegans aren't always amazing people

However, it seems that humans can't help but act like humans and this will inevitably result in problems at community events. As much as we love to think of ourselves as living on a higher level, vegans are not an exception. When you take on the task of bringing people together, you also take on the responsibility of keeping attendees safe. I have always used a safer space policy for events I organise and I try my very best to enforce these rules of engagement. One of the most difficult times I've experienced as a vegan community organiser was when I attempted to tackle the problem of men being aggressive and pushy with women during London Vegan Drinks.

I wrote what I thought was an irreverent yet firm 'don't do this sort of thing' article on my blog and shared it with all attendees. Can you guess what happened? Some advice I might give you would be to not write anything online calling out men on their behaviour if you want a trouble-free existence. Of course I was inundated with abuse, claims that I was trying to ruin romance, and even an attempted boycott of all future events I had anything to do with because I was anti-man. One guy showed up at my event and physically threatened me because I had insulted his masculinity and divine right to do whatever the hell he wanted around women without any recourse.

It was frightening and upsetting during the aftermath, but what made it bearable was the fact that the vegan community we had been cultivating circled around and stood up for what was the right thing to do. A pat on the back was much more powerful than an abusive email. Women who had stopped coming to the monthly meetings and socials started showing up again. Mixed groups would welcome new arrivals together instead of single men moving in like vultures. A handful of men even commented on how they could now see that their behaviour was oppressive or could be making women uncomfortable. We created a vibrant and caring community and the community pulled together when it needed to.

NON-VEGANS ALSO WELCOME

Another important aspect of community-centric events is that they can act as effective vegan outreach. A fun event is a fun event, whether it is vegan or not. People who are curious about how they can help to improve outcomes for animals are able to explore the concepts around veganism in an informal and fun situation. A powerful way to make veganism accessible is to make people feel valued and celebrated at community events even if they are not yet vegan.

When I run the huge London Vegan Beer Fest each year, I like to try and estimate or determine how many non-vegans come to the event. To the best of my ability, I put the figure at around 40 per cent of attendees at this large vegan event not being vegan. This is an incredible opportunity to spread the message of veganism in a fun, accessible and non-threatening manner. We are not telling people they are wrong for not being vegan, we are simply showing them what a heck of a good time they can have if they make the change.

A warm and protective community is one of the most powerful tools when it comes to helping people go vegan and stay vegan. A friend of mine who I met through London Vegan Drinks was a vegetarian for the first few years of attending the event and would make no secret of the fact that she had no interest in turning vegan. After not seeing her at a few events, she suddenly reappeared one month to declare that she had made the switch to veganism. Of course we were all thrilled for our friend and her decision, but she was more staggered that we had not tried to make her feel ashamed of not being vegan all of the time we knew her! She had finally made a deep and profound connection between her food choices and how animals suffer and she wanted to know why we had been so nice to her for so long! We had always been there, not judging but ready with information and support if she needed to access it, but she needed to get there in her own time. She now says she would never go back to non-vegan living and her acceptance into our vegan community before she had even committed to the lifestyle surely had a massive impact on her decision to see it as a viable and valuable decision.

VeGaNiSM iS a BROaD CHURCH

So building a supportive and inclusive community is hugely valuable for a number of reasons, but it's also important to understand why minorities need to socialise and organise on individual terms within broader vegan circles. Those who share specific experiences benefit from creating events and spaces together, and those of us who don't belong to these groups need to understand that sometimes we have a responsibility to step away.

As we discussed in a previous chapter, the forces that oppress people in broader society also exist within vegan communities. It is necessary and beneficial for a minority to find safe spaces in which they can celebrate and explore veganism without the people who sometimes take on the role of the oppressor. One very clear example of this is when you notice a women-only group or event in your area. Women choose to gather in women-only spaces for extremely valid reasons including systemic misogyny as a whole and individual anti-social behaviour directed at them at large scale social events.

I started a social group a few years ago for LGBTQ+ vegans in the London area. This group sprung forth from a real need to resist heteronormative and homophobic situations within the London vegan scene. Vegan social events and food fairs often showcase speed-dating events catering solely to heterosexual, cis-gendered men and women. As in all realms of society, there are of course people attending vegan events who voice the opinion that marriage should be between a man and a woman, that trans people should not be entitled to protective laws, and that 'non-traditional' relationships should be hidden behind closed doors.

This support group is still going strong long after I stopped being directly involved and it is wonderful to see regular get-togethers advertised. For some members, these outings are the only opportunities they get to feel celebrated for their veganism while not having to deal with the draining realities of a world that is unfriendly towards queers.

As you start to find a vegan community to involve yourself in, look for niche vegan groups if you feel you will benefit from them, share information about them with friends who you believe would enjoy knowing about them, and get the facts straight in your head on just why minority support groups within vegan circles are necessary. Use these facts to explain to other vegans who might think it is a form of preferential or discriminatory treatment. Let them know that oppressed people don't stop being oppressed just because they are hanging out with other vegans. Safe spaces are needed to socialise, organise and politicise. They are needed for people to take time out from the hugely daunting reality of living in an often-hostile world and to explore veganism on their own terms.

BUILDING COMMUNITY

Community is not all about vegan beer fests and eating as much as you can at a potluck. We vegans also need to take action for other members of our community in order to foster solidarity and resist oppression. That might result in you having to extend yourself into situations that don't directly benefit you personally, but being part of a healthy community is sometimes watching your neighbours succeed or be lifted up instead of you.

If you vote in local and national elections, one of the best ways you can help your community is by not voting for politicians with oppressive agendas or policies. Of course we often look for candidates with the most progressive policies around animal welfare such as members of the European parliament who have been vocal in their support of laws to stop the testing of cosmetics on animals, but we need to also back representatives who are interested in protecting our health and disability services, pushing for fair wages, abolishing damaging working contracts, showing compassion for refugees, bolstering public education and protecting the natural environment.

Some of these campaigning issues might feel disconnected from veganism in your mind, but I can assure you that even as a vegan I have required hospitalisation and education. I have needed lawful protection as a gay person and as a worker. Politicians voting to take away your public services are not doing anything positive for your vegan communities – so you need to look for government representatives with an interest in protecting every human. Strong vegan advocacy can only spring forth from strong, united communities and we can help shape such a world by entrusting our political landscape with inclusive and progressive representatives.

If you can afford to do it, donate money or time towards helping independent businesses set up in your area. The entire community benefits from having vibrant, useful and progressive independent businesses in its midst. Money made by a local business is then spent in your community, helping to stabilise and support your area. Look for fundraising campaigns designed to help cover the costs associated with setting up a new business and give funds if you are able. If you can send money further afield, consider supporting small vegan business in countries or regions with less opportunity. You don't have to limit acts of community to strengthening your own community.

Give back to your community by attending locally organised events that have an emphasis on supporting independent business. If you are able to offer time, volunteer at them: you will be helping organisers keep costs lower, you will meet members of your community and you will be an active participant and not just a passive bystander. Use whatever means you have at your disposal to spread news of local vegan events whether that be word of mouth, offering to distribute flyers, or posting on social media. Do these things even if you know you can't make it to a specific event. A fun, vibrant and inclusive event is all about developing social capital for the people around you and you have a big part to play in the process.

Look to help vegans in your area even if it's not a vegan problem they need help to solve. It sounds hokey and dripping with feel good sentimentality, but be prepared to offer your support to people you meet and try to resist the notion of only looking out for your immediate friends and family. Individuals you encounter within vegan circles will all have varying social, emotional and financial strains and stresses. If you can assist to lighten one person's load, you are actively strengthening your community. Helping others is in your best interest.

I feel that a vegan community really shows its true power when it unites to do good outside of the narrow constraints of veganism, just as we've seen with other minority social justice groups raising their voices for causes outside of their own, such as Lesbians and Gays Support the Miners during the 1980s miners' strike. By the time you read this book, I will have raised money via my vegan beer events around the UK to help support the work carried out by Mexico City-based Isla Urbana. Isla Urbana goes into communities in need to install desperately required water collection systems in homes and schools throughout some of the most economically disadvantaged neighbourhoods of the Mexican capital. These areas are often completely cut off from services such as clean drinking and cooking water even, a basic human right that the vast majority of people within the UK enjoy.

Vegans shouldn't just care about not eating animals, and our compassion is more convincing and powerful when it is not limited. I asked members of UK vegan communities who came to my beer events to extend their compassion in a small way to people living in Mexico without water. The collective power of the people at these beer events was directed to benefit people on the other side of the world. There is an important takeaway about community in this example and that is an effective, united and empowered community works to improve outcomes for their own members as well as contributing to wellness and equitable outcomes on a global scale.

Community is less about achieving victories for the individual and more about everyone being in it together. It goes against what we are told by politicians and mainstream media, but you honestly don't need to be the richest person in the room to be happy. Joy and fulfilment will come from feeling loved, supported and respected by your community. Your worth as a human does not stand apart from what you can contribute to all the various communities to which you belong, vegan or otherwise.

Consider what value or long-term happiness you can sustain as a vegan activist if people in your community cannot afford to pay their bills. How will you be an effective campaigner against suffering if elected politicians get to work to close hospitals or strip away affordable health care? The broader community in which you exist is in turn the bedrock of your vegan communities. You have a responsibility to nurture and champion all communities of which you are a member, as well as other communities on the planet to which you do not belong. Improved outcomes for animals, humans and the planet can only be achieved by dedicating yourself to building communities that support all human and non-human wellbeing.

Recharge and Refuel

I actually can't believe how exceptionally vegan I'm getting for this pit stop but I need to discuss a particular word with you. Kale. This cruciferous vegetable is often the punch line in jokes about gentrification and veganism, but believe me when I tell you it is one of the most versatile ingredients you will learn to love as a vegan.

Throw some fresh kale into a food processor with nutritional yeast, sea salt and a handful of almonds for an impossibly tasty green pesto that can be stirred through cooked pasta or spread on toast.

If you are feeling the need for a crunchy snack, roll kale leaves in a tiny amount of olive oil and dust with onion and garlic powder (and some chilli for the heat lovers) before baking on a low heat until the leaves turn into crunchy chips.

CHAPTER SiX

VEGAN TRAVEL

> We can travel without relying on animal products, we can be mindful of our surrounds, and we can consider how we interact and respect cultures and societies in which we are outsiders.

Up to this point, we've been concerned with exploring the reasons why you might want to be vegan as well as how you can be a decent vegan. I understand the road so far has included a lot of me telling you what you should do and why you should feel bad for not doing more. Apologies for any perceived bad vibes and or uncomfortable feelings.

Actually, forget that. I've changed my mind about your hurt feelings. Everything we have discussed is crucial and you are just going to have to deal with the confrontational feelings conjured up. Isn't that the most fabulous part of growing as a person? The more confronting a realisation, the more you probably need to take it on board for your own personal growth.

Well, you're welcome. I'm here to help.

I do however understand that I might not have you with me until the final pages of this book if I carry on relentlessly in sassy schoolteacher mode for another few chapters, so I'm going to take my chubby foot off my sanctimonious pedal for a short while as I explore the wonderful world of vegan travel for your enjoyment. If you are revelling at the insights into social justice and how to resist multiple oppressions as a vegan, don't fear. I'll sneak a few in on the sly.

The approach to this chapter is of course greatly informed by my own experiences, including the luxury of having enough disposable income at certain times of my life to travel. I think it should be stated that I understand for the vast majority of people on the planet, travel for pleasure is not an option.

Travelling as a vegan has changed drastically over the past decade. I want to take these next few pages to explore some of the issues and improvements vegans face as we scuttle around the planet. Travel used to be an area in which we had to make a lot of sacrifices but as you will read, if you have the funds to move about as you please there is no reason why you can't do it from a vegan perspective.

Travel isn't simply a way to spend time you are not working doing something fun or relaxing, it is a valuable experience for broadening your understanding of the world, meeting new people, and developing your compassionate outlook. Crossing borders can open your eyes to what other people are going through, affording you an opportunity to reflect on how your individual choices impact people, the environment and animals all over the planet.

Some vegans, especially newbies, might feel a bit intimidated by the idea of visiting new cities and countries as a plant-based traveller. Managing interactions with restaurant servers in your hometown is one thing, but having to explain dietary restrictions in another language can be daunting. Language barriers can combine with anxieties about being out of your comfort zone to make even the most resilient vegan think twice about getting out into the great big world.

Like many areas of life, us vegans can make the experience of travelling less stressful and more welcoming by being prepared. Mitigate your concerns around language by arming yourself with common phrases outlining your vegan requirements. Pick travel destinations that are vegan friendly and travel with a plant-based buddy. The fulfilment you get from travelling can far outweigh the negatives. Be ready in advance and your veganism shouldn't get in your way of experiencing exciting new horizons.

ON THE ROAD

If you need proof of how much the world has swung in the direction of normalising veganism, have a look at inflight airline meals.

There was a time when a fourteen-hour flight from Australia to anywhere would result in nothing being offered by the airline. It was common practice to not serve any vegan options. I recall a funny-now-but-not-at-the-time story in which my partner Josh was ridiculed by cabin crew when asking for plant-based milk with his tea. The crewmember answered him with a laugh before calling down the cabin to co-workers by exclaiming, 'Can you believe this guy? Does he think we are a coffee shop?!'

Nowadays most major airlines have vegan inflight options, although this varies wildly and a vegan meal might not even be called a vegan meal. Just because a vegan meal has been requested and logged, don't assume you are actually going to end up with a fully plant-based dish in front of you. Of course, there are obvious mistakes such as butter instead of dairy free spread, but I've even found a tray of lamb chunks in gravy placed on my seat back tray table. Pay attention, do your best by ordering ahead, and always take back up supplies.

Online guides and smart phones have helped herald in a vegan travel revolution. I can recall travelling before the explosion of online guides and it wasn't exactly an environmentally friendly affair. Josh and I would print out pages and pages of MapQuest directions for every vegan place we had heard about, store them in a cardboard document wallet, and try to navigate from them whilst driving on freeways. Remember that scene from *Clueless* when they accidently drive on the freeway and they all scream? Yes, just like that, but papers detailing directions to eateries would also be flying about the car. Before the smart phone, we would discover vegan places by randomly driving past them. We became extremely adept at making a sharp turn if one of us spotted the 'V' word on a shop front.

As I mentioned earlier, Happycow is the most famous and most accessed online guide for vegan travellers. The site allows users to filter by region or city, as well as combing through for businesses that are a hundred per cent vegan. You can search for grocery stores, caterers, bakeries, restaurants, juice bars, delis, shoe stores, boutiques, hotels, bed and breakfasts and pretty much anything you might need or want while you are on the road. Barnivore is similar but focussed on alcohol – listing brands and breweries as well as wine, beer, cider, champagne and spirits from all over the world.

Both Happycow and Barnivore are user driven platforms, meaning you can add information and photographs to enrich the listings. It is the perfect opportunity for you to help fold back into these online traveller communities and add value to something that is also assisting you.

Vegan Vacations and Humane Holidays

If you are a vegan with more money than most, you can make use of the many specialised travel companies popping up around the globe. These businesses craft bespoke vacations and holiday experiences such as luxury fully vegan river cruises throughout Europe, raw food retreats in southeast Asia and hiking adventures through stunning terrain all over the planet.

While vegan cruising and luxury vacations are exciting developments for many vegans, the reality is that a lot of these travel options are out of reach of most people on the planet. Even with a well-paid job, the idea of spending a month's salary on a one-week trip is just not feasible for most of us reading this book.

However, the option is there and some people will be able to afford and justify the expense. I have travelled on a few of these cruises (working to promote them – I have a tight budget that wouldn't allow for such extravagance) and they are truly special experiences. We used to not even consider booking a cruise holiday for fear of not having anything to eat during our time on the water, so the joy on the faces of vegans who were historically locked out of such moments is truly eye opening.

KRISTINA DAWSON is in her mid-forties, has been vegan since February 2010 and was vegetarian all her life before that change. She lives in the northeast of England where vegan options are improving all the time.

'I enjoyed the vegan cruise out of Amsterdam I went on so much because I knew the majority of people were like-minded and I wouldn't be bombarded with the usual questions – I'm sure I don't need to include what they are. What I also liked about the cruise is the fact you can join in as little or as much as you like. You don't feel at all pressured.

> 'The best parts of a vegan-specific holiday are
> being provided with food without having to ask
> any questions (unless of course you have allergies/
> intolerances). Until I went on the cruise, I hadn't
> been abroad for over ten years, and since becoming
> vegan I had only gone on city breaks. I particularly
> love going to London as there are so many places to
> try. I have since been to Glasgow and Manchester,
> which were great and this year I am going to
> Sheffield for the first time. I sometimes use the
> Happy Cow app but prefer to get recommendations
> from friends.'

If you are in the position to take a vacation but you are
not in a position to spend a lot of cash, there are a few
approaches you can explore in order to have an enjoyable
break. Self-catering vacations are not only a great way
to make holidays more affordable, they also allow the
concerned vegan to take full control over meal planning.
I know it's fun to dine out but when you don't have the
funds, you do what you can. Spending a little bit extra
on an apartment with a small kitchen will mean you can
prepare all your meals in house, you get to eat exactly
what you want, and the money saved might just be the
difference between taking a vacation or staying at home.

A leap forward for vegan travellers with not a lot of disposable cash is house sitting. Entire websites are devoted to matching vacant houses with potential temporary guardians. Need a short explanation? A house owner or occupant needs to travel out of the city, state or country but they do not want to leave their house and/or companion animal unattended. You put your name forward and if accepted you stay for a few days, a few weeks or even months. There are opportunities for housesitting all over the planet so with a little planning ahead you can enjoy a tropical retreat or a bit of time checking out areas a few neighbourhoods away. As you will be in a home with full amenities, you can cook vegan cuisine to your heart's content.

Vegan camping makes for a more affordable holiday experience and I'm aware of community-driven vegan camping experiences in the UK, Australia and the USA. This is a great DIY alternative for people not wanting to negotiate housesitting services or who are looking for a more sociable experience and a way to make new friends. The basic premise involves a group of vegans finding a location, splitting the site hire costs, and sharing food and experiences in an outdoor setting. These shared camping vacations are lower cost and create opportunities for vegan families to interact in safe, child-friendly situations. If you can't find a vegan camping opportunity close to you, I highly suggest you start one of your own. It might only start small but you will be creating a much-needed resource for other vegans looking for affordable vacations. Don't forget everything we discussed in the community chapter!

I need to hold my chubby gay hands up at this point in the book and admit that so far I've paid no attention to the realities of young vegans or young people looking to explore their compassionate feelings for animals. Young people are often overlooked, not only within vegan circles, but also by the world in general. Adults like me are guilty of not affording adequate respect to the feelings and experiences of teenagers.

Thankfully, we have the wonderful group known as TeenVGN to make spaces in which young vegans are cherished, celebrated and listened to including one extremely wonderful vacation opportunity. They are more than picking up the slack created by uncaring older people such as me. TeenVGN is exactly what young vegan-curious need as well as being the sort of support group of which the world needs a lot more. The opportunity the group has created to experience a mini-break away from home within a vegan environment is the ultimate stepping stone for young vegans to begin thinking about how even travelling and vacations can be non-exploitative.

KYLie aND LauRa founded TeenVGN way back in 2013 as a social support group for young people including vegetarians, vegans and veg-curious teens. They aim to teach, educate and guide young people through their decision to live a compassionate lifestyle and give them the resources they need to spread these messages to their peers and the world. TeenVGN is non-profit as well as being volunteer run. All forms of donation are put directly into their website, awareness of the organisation and summer camp. Yes, a vegan summer camp for young folk.

The amazing duo of Kylie and Laura host and organise VGN Summer Camp – a five-night residential camp during the UK summer school holidays and possibly Europe's only residential vegan camp for teenagers. I asked Laura to explain what happens for the young people who attend the camp.

'The 2017 camp found us staying at a state of the art eco-friendly lodge with all of our catered meals being completely vegan. During the day, we ran workshops with campaign groups, talked about social justice issues and had lots of free time to hang out, make new friends, get creative and make space for the attendees to just enjoy the company of other compassionate young people.

'I think there is real value in these young people getting together at least once a year in a camp atmosphere as it's a quick way to make friends and it helps these young people realise that they aren't alone. They begin to understand that together they can be a stronger unified group of people. This encourages and empowers them, as well as fosters within them the desire to change the world. They leave camp feeling so connected to and fired up for the cause and we often hear wonderful stories from groups of friends who met at camp who go on to do great things around campaigning and getting involved in activism for the animals. It's so heartening for us to see them a few months later on social media, meeting up, organising and just spending time together.

'Camp is one hundred per cent accessible for young people with disabilities. We have specialist camp leaders who are trained in working with people with disabilities and it's always important for us to choose a venue that is accessible. We pride ourselves on being an inclusive, safe space for everyone. We've been fortunate enough to run a scholarship programme with [vegan elite marathon runner and activist] Fiona Oakes this year that allowed us to provide free spaces for two campers from low-income families. We hope that this is something we can continue to do by hopefully finding other patrons who feel encouraged to support these young people through scholarships and grants.'

TRAVEL LiKE YOU CARE

Just like every other action we take during our time on this planet, travelling results in impacts that can sometimes be damaging.

Travelling while respecting cultures, countries and people around the planet takes some thoughtful consideration. Just as we would in the areas and regions where we live, there are a lot of ethical issues we need to think through as we try to live vegan on the road. We need to not only work out the best way that we can lessen the suffering of non-human animals, we also need to ensure we are being mindful of what our travel actions are doing to the people and places we visit.

McDonald's. As a vegan, it's ironic that **RYAN PATEY** credits fast food as the start of the major events that led to where he is today, but it all makes sense if you ask him about it. Long story short, since flipping burgers in high school, Ryan has toured with and promoted numerous musicians, managed an all-ages venue, coordinated shows and festivals, created content for Discovery Networks and various other educational companies, published children's stories in South Korea, hosted talks at vegetarian conferences, moved far too many times, and started the vegan magazine, *T.O.F.U.*, which is read worldwide. Now, three years after quitting his full-time job as a copywriter with a web and marketing agency in 2014, Ryan is focusing his time on *T.O.F.U.* while housesitting and travelling as far as he can.

'I quit my full-time job at a digital marketing agency nearly three years ago, and within a month or so I was on a plane to Costa Rica. Since then, I've been hopping around the world on a limited budget while I try to create a sustainable income from *T.O.F.U.*, which is a vegan magazine I've been self-publishing since 2007. Although I've leaned on my credit card plenty, I've also spent far less than most people would expect given how much distance I've covered.

'One of the biggest secrets I have is that I house sit, and that's meant that most of my accommodation has been free. Plus, I've spent plenty of time with adorable critters in countries like Ireland, Greece, Turkey, Malaysia, Vietnam and more.

Although it's hard to get started, and I recognise it will not work well for folks with a set work schedule and major responsibilities, house sitting has been the key to my ability to travel cheaply.

'Outside of that, another trick is to work on your perception of what travelling means. If you're tied to the idea of a two-week vacation spent on a beach at a resort in some tropical place, then you're most likely going to need a big budget. However, if you spend some time researching cheaper destinations, you can stretch your money, which means more opportunities for food! Also, even just taking the time to explore the world around you without hopping on a plane can be a lot of fun. If you have access to a vehicle, just pick a spot on the map and go see what it's like. If you don't have a vehicle, then perhaps you can access public transit and see how far it goes? For me, travel is all about the chance to experience somewhere else in the world, and to see things in a different light. It doesn't have to come with a passport stamp. It can come with a conversation down the street from where you live.

'I've struggled with aspects of the question of how to travel respectfully of cultures, societies and realities for years, and I've never settled on a solid answer. The fact of the matter is that travel can never really be completely ethical. With that in mind, I think approaching travel in the same way that one approaches veganism is a good solution.

'Learn what you can about where you're going. Connect with locals, and listen to what they have to say. Respect their customs and be mindful of the fact that your country is only "normal" because you grew up there. Be careful of how you compare things, and try to avoid setting what you know as the standard. It may be to you, but for billions of other people, something else is normal.

'Along with this, research the places you're thinking about spending your money at. Whether this is sanctuaries, accommodations, tour guides, restaurants, or something else, if you wouldn't set foot in a Wal-Mart at home, trying to avoid them somewhere else is probably a good idea.

'Personally, the big debate I've always had with myself (and others) is around spending money while travelling. Chances are, you're going to stand out in some of the places you find yourself in, and that means it's very possible that you'll pay a higher price for something or receive more attention from someone because you'll be seen as having more money than the locals. Although this is most likely true in plenty of parts of the world if you're able to simply pop in to see the sights and then head back home a couple weeks later, the implications of either paying the higher prices or arguing for lower ones are complicated. On the one hand, your money is supporting someone (and possibly their family), and the price you pay is probably significantly higher than their usual income. However, by paying this price you're also encouraging business owners to attend to your needs instead of the locals, and you're promoting services and goods that only tourists can afford. Sure, being able to eat gluten-free pancakes with no oil might be nice while watching the sun set on the beach, but is it worth the community losing their local cantina just for your two-week vacation? I can think of plenty of examples of this, especially in places like Chiang Mai, Thailand, and I've had conversations with locals who weren't sure of the right answer either.

'Overall, I just try to do what feels right, but I also don't have the money to spend in fancier places, so my wallet typically keeps me in line even when my stomach just wants waffles and chocolate smoothies without the socio-economic complications.'

Travelling prepared as a vegan is not something I suggest lightly – it is a straight up necessity. You can save yourself a lot of stress and hungry times by putting things in place and thinking ahead. I have discovered that planning food stops, asking about vegan options ahead of time, and even carrying my own pantry staples on some occasions has saved me a lot of unnecessary grief. You wouldn't want to spend a week on the road with a hungry Fat Gay Vegan. It's not a pretty or enjoyable situation.

If you travel for work and have a say in where you get to stay, call or email ahead of time to explain your requirements to your host hotel. A simple document outlining what vegan means that also features some basic meal ideas that any chef or kitchen hand could follow is a valuable tool. It might feel a little passive aggressive but those feelings will not seem so important if you find yourself in the middle of a business conference with nothing to eat but apples washed down with sparkling water.

This reaching out in advance is advice I also offer up to anyone travelling for pleasure. If you are fortunate enough to be in a financial position to pay for travel, you can sure as heck tell the people you are paying what you want to eat or that you choose to abstain from animal products. It would be an extremely rare occurrence that you would find yourself in a resort as a paying guest where the management do not want to make simple changes to make your stay more enjoyable. Speak with the chef. Make your concerns heard. Flex your compassionate consumer muscle.

This might sound a bit trite, but pack snacks for journeying. Flights get delayed and roads snowed in. You do not want to find yourself in an airport lounge with only crisps and soda as sustenance for an eight-hour unplanned layover. Forgotten inflight meals (which happens more than you would imagine) won't be an issue when you have pre-packed sandwiches, energy bars, dried fruit and nuts, plus mini plant-based milks for tea and coffee. Packing your own food is also the only guaranteed way you are going to like what you are eating on a plane.

If you're a seasoned vegan traveller you may have been rolling your eyes throughout this chapter and want to give me stern talking to about stating the obvious. But we can't forget that we were not all vegan from the minute we landed on earth and many people reading this book are just joining us. These tips, insights and considerations will hopefully assist the new vegan during their globetrotting and maybe, just maybe, the chapter will help convince an almost-vegan reader that their regular life of socialising and journeying around the globe doesn't haven't to end if they make the switch to a more compassionate lifestyle.

We can travel without relying on animal products, we can be mindful of our surrounds, and we can consider how we interact and respect cultures and societies in which we are outsiders. Take time to get used to what travelling vegan means to you and try not to put yourself in situations that are going to be too difficult. Use the guides that exist and help build them if you have the time and expertise. Just because you are on the road doesn't mean you are on your own. Vegans all over the planet have got your back.

MY TOP VEGAN CITIES

If you possess the means to travel, here is my list of ten vegan destinations on the planet around which you might want to plan future vacations. Of course, things can change rapidly in the vegan universe, so this guide is more a rough overview to cities that have been historically accommodating to vegans. Basically, if you find yourself in any of these locations you are going to not feel hard done by as a compassionate traveller.

LONDON

If you had asked me five years ago if London should be on this list of top global destinations for vegans, I would have said no. Or maybe I could have been convinced to allow it to just scrape in. Now the city gets a resounding inclusion. The UK capital is absolutely overflowing with vegan businesses, including grocery stores, pizza restaurants, shoe boutiques, street food traders and even a compassionate hair salon. I'm not going to sugar coat the tough truth about price, however. London can be one of the most expensive places to visit as a tourist and you will often find yourself startled by the cost of local transport, accommodation and even vegan groceries and snacks.

Paris

The French capital has also come on in leaps and bounds regarding vegan tourism. You can dine in exquisite restaurants serving fine French cuisine, shop in a plant-based supermarket on a self-catering vacation, or stroll the city's avenues while munching on a vegan hot dog and fries. The vegan-ness of this gorgeous city keeps expanding and it is a wonderful destination for the compassionate traveller.

Barcelona

Not only is Barcelona one of the most visually stunning cities on the planet, it is one of the places in which vegan food is most readily accessible. Check listings for the latest vegan hotspots and investigate vegan grocery stores scattered around the city. Restaurants and cafés catering to vegans love to veganise Spanish and regional Catalonian dishes, so there is no need to miss out on tastes of the region just because you live a vegan lifestyle.

MEXICO CITY

The Mexican capital is a megacity that has shocked me by how rapidly it has become one of the top vegan destinations on the planet. When I first visited back in 2008, I could not locate one single vegan restaurant. Visitors now enjoy more options than they could possibly narrow down. High-end eateries, street stands serving tacos, and everything in between all wait for the vegan tourist. Shop in one hundred per cent vegan grocery stores and attend the multiple vegan food fairs that take place around the city throughout the year.

LOS ANGELES

Southern California has always been a hot spot for vegan food. I recall visiting for the first time back during 1999 and being bowled over by the bizarre ease with which you could locate vegan food. From 1970s-style health food stores in the Valley to blissed out plant-based burger joints by the beach, LA has long been a top destination for vegans. This becomes even more the case with every passing year with an almost intimidating number of vegan food businesses spread out in every corner of the city.

San Francisco

The Bay Area has long been a vegan paradise, but recent years have enjoyed even a wider range of plant-based eating on offer. Stunning comfort food, Mexican dishes, cinnamon rolls dripping in frosting, and burger options for miles all make San Francisco a top destination. It is worth noting that Berkeley and Oakland across the water have extremely vibrant vegan scenes.

Sydney

I haven't visited Sydney in years but reports flowing out of the harbour city have me believing I am missing out on a grand scale. A gelato and ice cream store recently switched to a one hundred per cent vegan menu and you can fill up around the Australian city on 'fish' and chips, pizza, raw cuisine and more. Get into the local specialty of pies with mashed potato and peas covered in gravy.

New York City

If you are a vegan visiting NYC and you don't feel overwhelmed by the sheer number of vegan dining options, you mustn't have seen the full list. The city is swarming with plant-based food and you don't have to stop there. Fill your wardrobe with vegan shoes and outfits, mine radical bookstores for animal rights titles, and get to the outer boroughs for some of the best plant-based eating on the planet.

Warsaw

If you have been to Warsaw recently, you'll know all about the vegan revolution that has swept through the Polish city. If you haven't had the pleasure of visiting, open up an online guide to vegan Warsaw and become speechless at what surely must be one of the largest collections of one hundred per cent vegan businesses in any country. When it comes to the number of vegan eateries per capita, Warsaw might very well be the most vegan place on the planet.

Taipei

The Taiwanese city is almost intimidating when it comes to the sheer scope of totally vegan eateries lining its streets. Take a trip to the Happycow online guide, search for Taiwan, and marvel at the number of restaurants and cafés. There are a number of outlets of the international chain of vegan comfort food restaurants called Loving Hut, plus dozens of independent businesses that would take weeks to work through. Taiwan appears to be a vegan food lover's paradise.

BERLiN

If you want to experience vegan saturation, plan a visit to
Berlin. Even for the plant-based consumer who believes
they have seen everything, Berlin comes as a shock. The
city is overflowing with vegan food choices and I actually
feel real sorrow for the traveller with a mere two days to
explore everything on offer. If you need vegan ice cream
parlours, fancy patisseries, all-you-can-eat brunch buffets,
shoe stores, delicatessens, coffee shops, high-end restaurants
or fast food joints, Berlin is the city you need to visit.

NOTaBLE MENTiONS

There is not enough space in this book to list every
vegan-friendly city on the planet. I need to get back
to sanctimonious posturing. Before I do, I would like
to give a shout out to some cities that were almost
included in the above list. Make time for Budapest if
you are interested in gorgeous Hungarian food, check
out Portland, Oregon to see how veganism can ingratiate
itself into all walks of life, take a break in Melbourne
for a vegan culture experience Down Under but with a
European café feel, marvel at the huge number of vegan
bars and live music venues in Glasgow, and eat some of
the best food on the planet in Philadelphia.

Recharge and Refuel

Mexican cuisine is something I recommend new vegans explore if they are unfamiliar. So many of the staples of Mexican kitchens are vegan friendly, with corn and beans featuring heavily. One of my treats involves potato, cooked black beans, vegan cheese, corn tortillas, and some very hot oil for frying. Taquitos will be your new best friends. Make a mixture of mashed potato, beans and shredded vegan cheese, taking a few risks with added ingredients that are suited to your tastes. Diced serrano chilli, finely chopped white onion, or a smattering of roasted garlic chunks will give the mixture a bit of extra flair. Take a spoonful of the mixture and spread onto a corn tortilla. Roll the tortilla into a long cylindrical tube and fry (in just enough hot oil to cover) until crunchy. A pro tip is to make use of wooden skewers to stop your taquitos from opening up in the hot oil. You can thread three taquitos onto one skewer for faster cooking. Serve hot taquitos with your favourite salsa and a side of shredded cabbage for a taste sensation.

CHAPTER SEVEN

THE FUTURE OF VEGANISM

> Be unapologetically vegan and do it with kindness, compassion and understanding.

Throughout this book I've unpacked what veganism means in general, what it means to me on a personal level, and how to practically and ethically apply it to the world in which we live. We have explored what it means to make the decision to live a vegan life and how these choices can impact on people around you.

But what does the future hold for veganism?

How are our independent vegan businesses going to expand and survive in a world hurtling full throttle into the land of seemingly irreversible big business? How do we as activists make decisions that benefit humans and animals? Can we successfully challenge and resist racism, sexism and ableism within our movement while actively working to improve outcomes for animals? In what ways will we be able to keep animals as the underpinning idea of what it means to choose a vegan lifestyle?

This chapter is a chance for us to imagine what might come next. Whether you are a long-term vegan or somebody just about to start this exciting, compassion-expanding chapter of your life, it is important to consider exactly what part you might play in this global movement. Of course, we cannot know for certain how the world will change and to what level veganism will be shaped to fit our modern societies, but I'm willing to offer up a little conjecture and speculation for you all.

Independent vegan businesses are surely set to go from strength to strength as we move into the future if we support them. In the not too distant past, a one hundred per cent vegan establishment was a rarity in a lot of parts of the world but they are becoming increasingly common. The commercial viability of running vegan businesses can be seen all over the planet and is a result of not just the huge increase of people committing to a vegan lifestyle, but also the number of non-vegans comfortable with veganism being another type of cuisine. This will only increase as vegan visibility continues to gain traction in the media and vegan lifestyle activist groups push forward with outreach work.

We can expect to see even more vegan chain restaurants, supermarkets and business success stories, such as Veganz grocery stores in Europe, fast-casual USA restaurants Veggie Grill and By Chloe, or clothing, food and household emporium The Cruelty-Free Store, which is spreading across state capitals in Australia. These businesses are absolutely booming and the more the general public encounter them, the more comfortable they will become shopping with them.

Of course, these businesses are succeeding within a capitalist framework, as discussed previously in this book, meaning it is our duty as inclusive vegans to demand fair business practices from them even as we support them. We need to let businesses know we expect them to pay living wages to all employees, offer health and insurance benefits, and put environmentally sound strategies in place. We need to demand that our vegan businesses do better in all areas as we help them achieve world domination. They need to help improve outcomes for animals as well as the people making their success possible, from workers in their own store to workers all along the supply chain.

The future success of smaller independent vegan business will rely in a large part on collaboration. Just as groups of retailers, traders and professionals have done ever since there has been organised commerce, vegan business owners will find strength in joining forces. It makes sense to work together to protect the collective interests of vegan businesses and workers, such as lobbying local authorities for incentives that encourage and support more environmentally friendly endeavours.

Local business and trade groups can also be valuable by sharing helpful information with start-ups. Setting up a new business in any field is tough so insider knowledge about laws, legislation, tax codes and established community groups and vegan bloggers can make life that little bit easier. Imagine a world where you didn't have to start the business learning curve from scratch on top of working incredibly anti-social hours? Groups for vegan businesses are starting to pop up all over the planet. I was fortunate enough to be at the first meeting of one such business owners' association in Glasgow, Scotland. It is a powerful tool when people come together for the greater good and it is one of the keys to the advancement of vegan business.

A final note on this collaborative approach to business is the importance of cross promotion. Vegan businesses can shout out other vegan businesses on their social media platforms, making sure everyone is getting the most out of their efforts. Companies can team up to split advertising costs, especially in the case of non-competitive businesses. If a vegan business needs a graphic designer, they could consider hiring a vegan graphic designer to feed back into the vegan business community. The same can be said for vegan PR specialists, vegan event planners, vegan accountants and almost any other professional a business might require or engage.

The future of veganism also means an ever-evolving social media landscape in which we promote, socialise, politicise and campaign.

We'll see a rise in activists and personalities utilising social media to disseminate their version or understanding of veganism and there is a crucial need to celebrate and share the views of these people. Marching forward as a vegan collective into an uncertain future, we should be supporting these online activists when we can by sharing their content and financially backing the important outreach they carry out in the name of veganism. Ask your favourite vegan content creators how they need your help to carry on spreading the message and then do what you can to help them. This need to support and elevate vegan voices becomes even more crucial when the activists and personalities belong to minorities currently sidelined in vegan circles. Need a refresher on what the heck I'm talking about? Skip back a few chapters. I'll grab a drink and a snack while you are gone and meet you back here in a moment or two.

Great. Welcome back. I'm glad you've reminded yourself of why it is important that we centre traditionally oppressed voices within our vegan message. The future of our movement as vegans and our planet as humans relies on us doing this very thing.

For many years vegans have relied on social media pages and online forums to share news of accidentally vegan products. You know what accidentally vegan means, right? A lot of food, products and clothing that are suitable for vegans aren't marketed as such because the manufacturers hadn't considered that angle. The products just by chance don't include any animal derived ingredients or components, meaning resourceful vegans track them down and share details with their communities.

In the future, I predict we will see a surge in companies making slight changes to their products to bring them in line with vegan expectations. The demand is there now and we are already seeing it happen. In 2017 we saw this occur in record time when an alcoholic beverage company (that shan't be named because I don't want to play favourites or ruin any future chances of six-figure FGV sponsorship deals with competitors) released a non-dairy version of a world-famous drink only to be met by a sea of angry vegans complaining about a honey-derived ingredient. Yes, the honey was the only thing stopping the drink from being vegan. The company responded swiftly by delaying the launch of the product until they could ensure it was completely vegan-friendly.

This re-release of an almost vegan product took place just before I sat down to write this chapter with the well-known frozen and chilled meat free company, Linda McCartney. The company upset vegans (can you see a pattern here with our temperaments? Ha! Just kidding – we are totally adorable) by releasing an imitation pulled pork burger made from vegetable protein but again made unsuitable for plant eaters by the inclusion of honey. Look, if I got cash every time honey ruined a vegan party I'd be brunching with Alicia Silverstone and her child Bear Blu in some fancy vegan café in West Hollywood. Funny aside, now you know how I'd live if I were rich. Tell everyone you know to buy this book and I promise to keep you all updated of my antics via Instagram.

Linda McCartney bosses seemed to take the criticism seriously as we now have a honey free version of the burger on supermarket shelves around the UK and mainland Europe. This phenomenon is set to really start rollicking along over the next few years as companies begin to understand just how many hundreds of thousands of customers (millions if they are a global brand) they are alienating by not going that extra step to veganise a product that is almost there anyway. People who are answerable to the bottom line are really starting to open their eyes to the profit-making opportunities going begging by stopping at vegetarian when in reality, vegetarians, vegans and animal consumers can all buy vegan stuff.

As tomorrow becomes today, we will continue to see the rush by non-vegan restaurants and businesses to make notable efforts to include vegan products for profit. Huge restaurant chains with locations numbering in the hundreds have been busy over the past few years adding vegan menu items and even going as far as offering stand-alone vegan menus for guests. UK giants such as Zizzi and Pizza Express have already committed to the inclusion of vegan menu items in a big way, with Zizzi even featuring a sizeable vegan wine list. Pret a Manger is a retail chain specialising in gourmet sandwiches that opened a meat free outlet in central London, and, shortly before I sat down to write this book, the company was more than happy to announce the biggest sellers in this specialised location were the vegan offerings. In addition to opening a second meat-free London store, Pret a Manger has even announced a plan to roll out meat-free fridges in their non-vegetarian outlets, showing the clear buying power compassionate consumers are able to wield. I've even been in multiple restaurants within Las Vegas casinos where vegan cuisine is offered readily across menus.

One of the biggest barriers facing new and developing vegan business is the realities of small scale production which results in the need to charge more at the point of sale, which in turn sees lower sales figures when compared to non-vegan products. We are beginning to see the tide turning when it comes to economies of scale, meaning businesses are experiencing the lower production costs available to them as the demand increases for vegan products. The more they make and the more they sell, the lower the 'per product' costs will be and the more affordable they can make their goods for the consumer.

This will become more apparent in the near future but we are already seeing vegan shoe companies selling footwear at competitive prices, vegan frozen food companies supplying affordable products into mainstream retailers, and even purposively vegan beer brands at regular retail price points. As demand for vegan goods and services increases, this competitive capacity by businesses to compete in the market place alongside non-vegan companies will become unstoppable until the lines are hardly recognisable.

The runaway success of veganism as a commodity with a strong bottom line means we are going to see vegan brands being bought out by multinationals who are keen to get a piece of the action. We've already seen this happening in traditionally solid industries that are now recognising the rising market share of the plant-based sector (and they are most definitely feeling the heat). Dairy companies all over the planet are pouring investment money into dairy-free alternatives and we already have supermarkets all over the planet that are stocked with vegan cheese and milk products owned by companies that only a few years ago were only packaging and selling cow-derived foods.

A dairy producer called Elmhurst in Queens, New York went a step further in 2017. This 90-year-old dairy completely abandoned its cow milk production and now exclusively produces and sells plant-derived milks, such as cashew, almond and walnut milks. Using Elmhurst, one of the biggest dairy producers on the USA's east coast, as precedent we can expect to see more about-faces by big business over the coming years. As lifestyle trends change and consumers awaken to the welfare, environmental and health problems associated with consuming and buying animals, companies that are used to making a lot of money will take these opportunities to stay on top.

The explosion we are experiencing when it comes to plant-based alternatives will result in kick back from big business when it comes to the naming of products. Dairy and meat producers are taking time out from using animals for profit to lobby government departments around the globe, asking them to protect words such as milk, sausages and cheese from being used to name or market plant-based foods in an attempt to hinder the growth of the animal-free sector. In 2016 a mayonnaise company even started legal proceedings against a big name vegan mayonnaise producer. The non-vegan company was definitely feeling threatened by the plant-based mayo and tried legal channels to put a halt to their use of any terms relating to mayo. The vegan company prevailed but I don't think this is the last we will see of these types of challenges. People make a lot of money from farming and killing animals. They will do what they can to protect their profit margin.

Activists will continue to push supermarkets and producers for clearer vegan labelling on packaging. Shoppers have seen an immense increase in store own-brand labelling across the planet with many major retailers even producing vegan product lists for customers to download online. Consumer advocacy groups will continue to lead this charge and individual vegan shopper feedback will make a difference at local levels. We fill in those customer feedback cards enough times and they listen. I promise.

The UK-based Vegan Society will continue to spread its trademark scheme in all markets and countries. The programme is surely the most instantly recognisable vegan-labelling programme on the planet. Businesses register and are vetted by the Society for any products they sell that are suitable for a vegan lifestyle. Once approved, the small vegan logo can be displayed on packaging and labels as an unmistakable mark of recognition for vegan shoppers.

As big business and retailers clamour for vegan money over the next few years, I predict we will see a record number of products carrying the trademark logo from The Vegan Society as well as any one of the copycat trademark schemes popping up in different regions. Business likes to take out any unnecessary steps in order to achieve a sale and for vegans the biggest obstacle is identifying a product as animal-free. I think we are only seeing the beginning of how important these vegan logos will become in the relationship between the money makers and the spenders.

Prepare yourself for an onslaught of news reports detailing mind-boggling financial investments in vegan enterprise over the next decade. Many investors see veganism as the next big return, meaning larger amounts of money and capital are set to be invested into ground breaking vegan developments. However, I do believe the main driver behind these investments will be more the environmental ramifications and less about the animals.

We have already seen tech and self-made digital millionaires and billionaires pumping vast sums of capital into vegan egg alternatives, lab-grown meat and all manner of vegan food development. You need a firm grasp on accountancy to break down some of the amounts of money that have been put into big name vegan brands such as Beyond Meat and Hampton Creek.

I do hold fears for the loss of our vegan communities as acceptance of the term and the lifestyle marches seemingly unwaveringly into the mainstream. It is wonderful to see such a broad embrace of a compassionate choice but we are in danger of losing the quirky uniqueness cultivated by our potlucks and village fêtes and fairs. We have been so dependent for so many decades on our secret little groups and meetings that I think some of us would be lost with these lines of support.

But even though veganism is becoming just another type of cuisine for a lot of people, I still believe we can still develop and nurture niche support groups. As we've talked about, there is so much more we get from these connections than just getting to hang out with other vegans. We should be making spaces for vegan women, LGBTQ+ vegans, vegans of colour, vegans living with disabilities, business vegans, vegans who love country walking, nightlife-obsessed vegans, vegans with children, and any other type of vegan you can imagine. The people within our movement will be more effective advocates for veganism if we push for ways to celebrate every part of who they are as individuals. Start a vegan social group. It's the future of our strong communities.

In the Netflix-exclusive film *Okja*, a multinational corporation starts a breeding program to create a new animal that can be used for food but that doesn't contribute to environmental problems to the level of other land mammals. The young protagonist of the film joins forces with an animal rights group to liberate one of the animals she befriends. I predict many more stories, publications, films and television shows dealing with improving outcomes for animals or, at the very least, explorations of how humans use and commodify non-human animals are to come. We will see art galleries dedicating space for shows dealing with animal rights and musicians releasing songs about the vegan lifestyle.

The line between vegan activist and businessperson or vegan celebrity will continue to blur. Over the past few years, we have seen the rise of celebrity plant-based chefs such as Chloe Coscarelli and restaurant chains built around people as brands. Expect this phenomenon to pick up steam as we move into the not-too distant future as YouTube personalities and bloggers team up with investment groups to capitalise on veganism as a product. Hey, maybe this book is an example of the very thing I'm talking about. Mainstream businesses such as publishers and content creators will continue to look for the next big vegan thing to help land a bestseller.

Possibly one of the most unexpected advancements over the coming years will be the growth in vegan professional sports teams. I was recently reading about the successes of vegan football club, Forest Green Rovers. This team from the UK town of Nailsworth recently came out on top of their division, meaning they will advance to playing in the English Football League Two for their next season. This is a remarkable achievement for a professional team in which all of the players eat a plant-based diet during season and not one non-vegan food item can be purchased in their stadium during games. News stories about the team's movement out of the National League into the higher bracket all made mention of the vegan angle, adding to the normalisation and mainstreaming of the lifestyle choice.

Of course, the main motivation behind the veganisation of sports teams such as Forest Green Rovers can be found in concerns for the environment and peak performance of the athletes. However, the recently formed Vegan FC in the northern Mexican city of Monterrey proves we will also see clubs and sporting groups putting the ethics of caring for animals at the heart of their endeavours. This Mexican football club is concerned with recruiting vegan players from the outset, not asking their current players to adopt a vegan diet.

We will see an increase in individual sports people adopting plant-based diets, as well as mainstream media incorrectly reporting this as veganism. While a lot of athletes focus on what a plant-based diet can do for improving their performance, many individuals are also exploring what their individual choices do for improving outcomes for animals. Put simply, an athlete eating only plants to enhance their personal best does not equate to them being a vegan. Rugby league player Anthony Mullally of UK team Leeds Rhinos has been extremely vocal in his choice to live a vegan life based on his desire to reduce harm to animals. Australian snooker champion Neil Robertson has also expressed his interest in exploring a vegan lifestyle after several years of eating a plant-based diet as a way to reach optimum form. I could go on but the list of athletes discovering ethical veganism is broad and rather exhausting.

As with the food served at the stadium of Forest Green Rovers, food for fans at sporting venues and events is set to become a bigger vegan issue in the future. You can already find vegan hot dogs at baseball stadiums around the USA and a quick Internet search will bring up dozens of user-created lists showing you how to eat vegan at a dazzling number of sporting and concert venues around the planet.

As we explored in the vegan travel chapter, life on the road for those wanting plant-based sustenance is improving and I believe we are set to see significant improvements. It stands to reason that the more we flex our compassionate consumer muscle, the more airlines will be willing to explore making vegan food available to passengers. In a 'you read it here first' moment, I expect a major airline to replace their vegetarian inflight option with completely plant-based menus very soon. It might have already happened by the time this book hits shelves. Not only is it a more inclusive policy to make the vegetarian meal a vegan option (everyone can eat vegan, only vegetarians and some animal eaters would choose to eat the vegetarian option), it makes complete financial sense. Why create an extra meal category when you can cover a lot of bases with vegan food? Airlines operate just like any other business looking to squeeze extra profit and I think we will see some fundamental changes to vegan food offerings based on the bottom line alone.

The vegan food expansion for travellers will not just be confined to eating in the air. Food on trains, ferries and other forms of transportation has already started to become more inclusive for vegans. A recent blog post guest written for me by a reader showcased a fancy three-course meal on a ferry company called Viking Line that runs between Stockholm and Helsinki. I've even ordered a hot vegan burger whilst travelling on a train down the Californian coastline. I honestly almost fell over when I saw a vegan burger option featured on the dining carriage menu.

The more vegans there are and the more money there is to be squeezed out of us, the more easily we will find vegan options on the road. If you travel by car throughout the UK, you'll be familiar with motorway services which are bizarrely frequent stopping points featuring low cost hotels, petrol stations and food courts. Traditionally, a motorway services stop was not something cherished by vegans as they have been known to be plant-based food wastelands, but things are looking up.

Train stations and airports are also places where vegan food availability is on the rise. It sounds like the stuff of vegan utopian dreams but there is actually a one hundred per cent vegan food outlet inside Terminal 4 of Los Angeles International Airport. Real Food Daily is a longstanding plant-based restaurant in Los Angeles with a couple of outlets, but the opening of a branch inside the airport sent seismic waves through the vegan world. Expect to see more of these sorts of vegan business placements in the future.

Take a few steps into the Eurostar's Brussels train terminal shopping mall and you will find a meat free café chain called Greenway Express serving seitan wraps and vegan burgers. Take the Eurostar back to London St Pancras and you will discover a vending machine inside the departure lounge that is packed solid with vegan snacks, drinks and food to go. This isn't a trend set to slow down anytime soon.

We have talked a lot about the future of vegan commerce (well, I have. You are very good listeners) but there is no future of vegan commerce unless we have effective and dedicated vegan activists leading the charge. Vegan activism must change and grow to stay effective and following are a few ways in which I think people around the world are going to do a great job of keeping animals at the centre of veganism.

In order to enact long-term advancement of vegan issues, we need to see activists and advocates making moves to enhance legislation to bring about stronger legal protections for animals. Real, fundamental change will come about through pressure on world governments and local authorities. There are a whole lot of people and companies around the globe who won't do the right things for animals unless they are told they have no choice. Our communities and our activists are becoming stronger as lobbyists and this will be a big area for growth for the vegan movement over the next decade. We need to be smart and we need to help shape the laws that protect animals.

Also, watch this space for more vegan politicians to be elected by their constituents.

In the UK, Parliament has enjoyed the company of multiple vegan politicians. This has included Kerry McCarthy, Cathy Jamieson and Chris Williamson as elected Members of Parliament, all of whom happen to be part of the Labour party. In the USA, you might have heard of New Jersey State Senator Cory Booker. Booker has been extremely vocal about the ethical underpinning of a vegan lifestyle, often talking about it on his social media accounts.

Vegan politicians obviously have more on their plate than just vegan issues, but having a vegan perspective inside the machinations of local and national politics is invaluable. Politicians have the opportunity to be a voice for animals when quite often there is simply no one else speaking up. As our movement starts to understand the importance of shaping policy in favour of non-human animals, expect to see a lot more vegans running for office.

Any conversation about the future of veganism must include the question of how ethical concerns will be embedded into our movement. The multiple oppressions affecting vegans will be challenged by vegan organisations and event spaces giving space to minority vegan voices. We will see a change in how our communities react to and respect different realities. As a brief example of how this can occur, the giant VegfestUK events around the UK have committed to the inclusion of talks, seminars and presentations focussing on resisting oppressive forces and practices within vegan communities. More and more vegans will start working to challenge and resist these oppressive forces that push vegans from the centre of the movement.

We become more effective in vegan campaigning when we work hard to be more inclusive and we make a better world when we are inclusive in our veganism. More of us will start to recognise how our own actions can contribute to the oppression of minority vegans and we will begin to understand how we can make changes to redress these situations. This ethical awakening is certainly not a quick destination to reach, rather an ongoing journey of expanded compassion to which we must all commit ourselves.

Groups such as Food Empowerment Project are working tirelessly to raise awareness of the human cost of food production, a fight in which many more vegan groups are becoming involved. When we spend money on products, we need to take responsibility and demand that the manufacturers and suppliers are paying fair wages, looking after worker health and insurance needs, as well as respecting the right of their employees to unionise. If we spend our money with companies that do not treat humans fairly, we are contributing to systems of oppression.

We all need to look for more consumer action groups of which we can be a part that will work towards pressuring business to consider the human cost of what they do, not just the non-human animal cost. Considering all forms of oppression when we make choices is becoming a more natural action and we will get better at this in years to come.

A big shift will start to occur when it comes to how much humans rely on industrialised farming of animals. This is a chipping away scenario that doesn't have an end. Rather, we are in a long-term battle for improved outcomes for animals, kindness and equity for humans, and a kinder world in general. Of course, some of the changes we are seeing when it comes to the mainstreaming of veganism seem breakneck, but nothing happening now or about to happen in the future is taking place without decades of hard work by dedicated activists, lobbyists and everyday vegans such as (hopefully) you and me.

We organise and attend local events that serve to celebrate existing vegans as well as encourage future vegans. Our money flows to independent vegan businesses to help keep them viable, while we also flex our compassionate consumer muscle to ensure vegan options in mainstream supermarkets and restaurants keep increasing. We work together to challenge racism, ableism, sexism, homophobia, classism, wealth disparity and inequity within our vegan communities. Our vocal and proud take on our veganism leads by example. There is no need to excuse it away or apologise. Be unapologetically vegan and do it with kindness, compassion and understanding.

To put it simply, you and I are the future of veganism. Let's get to it.

Recharge and Refuel

I'm not really known for eating raw food, so it might just come as a surprise to you that one of my favourite dishes is completely uncooked. I have my friend Julio Alcantara to thank for a whole lot of gorgeous food. Julio and I have made Mexican cooking videos together for a few years and we love feeding people together at our annual vegan Day of the Dead dinner party in London.

Many years ago, Julio introduced me to the simple and exquisite wonders of raw vegan ceviche. Take a bowl of button mushrooms and chop into quarters. Add half a red onion and one green chilli, both diced into small pieces. Liberally drench in fresh lime juice before adding coriander/cilantro, salt and pepper. I also cheekily add a squirt or two of ketchup before mixing well. Refrigerate for at least an hour to allow the raw ingredients to 'cook' in the lime juice. Serve as a side salad or with tortilla chips for a delicious snack. Another option to fill this dish out a bit more is to use fresh, diced tomato as well as some celery for extra texture and crunch.

CONCLUSION

> No matter how much we do, we can always do more
> and we can always do better.

You made it. Congratulations.

That's a lot of writing about how you can be a better person to digest and I appreciate that isn't always the sweetest pill to swallow. One of the toughest things to do as socialised and 'set in our ways' creatures is to take on board new ideas, especially if those ideas challenge how we already see our place in the world. I appreciate your attention to have made it through to the end of this book, and a bigger pat on the back to those who are yet to start your vegan journey. That is some open mindedness you got going on there, friend.

Of course, I hope you did more than just read the book and actually got something out of the chapters, but a real reward for me has been the journey the book took me on as I wrote it. If you are unsure about your feelings on a subject, I highly recommend writing 50,000 words about it. It's a sure-fire way to be confronted by your inner machinations and you will learn to see the bigger picture when it comes to how you and your own choices impact the world. The process of writing the book has been incredibly eye opening and a powerful way to re-establish a strong understanding of why I'm vegan and why I'm trying to make better choices for my community.

Laying out all my thoughts made me think deeply about why veganism is important to me. We don't often get the opportunity to think through our motivations to this level, let alone put them to paper and share with the world. Knowing that you would be reading this made me go over my approach to ethical living with a fine-toothed comb. What I was reminded of during this process was that the immovable and unquestionable goal of my veganism is to improve outcomes for non-human animals.

However, this book has reminded me of more than just my commitment to caring for the animals. Explaining the worldview of Fat Gay Vegan on these pages has made me see the part I play in the world on a much bigger scale. As a person interested in promoting compassion, I have a responsibility to listen to vegans who are not living the same reality to me. I have to take action to ensure I am not contributing to the oppression of humans, or at least recognise how my privilege is unavoidably contributing to these oppressions. I see clearly that I must choose ways to promote my veganism that do not negatively impact on other humans. Being tolerant of different realities to mine is not enough. It is my responsibility to be an active ally and work hard to redress and resist oppressive language, imagery and forces both in and out of my vegan circles.

Another important lesson I've laid out in this book is that no matter how much we do, we can always do more and we can always do better. This statement can at first seem terrifying but I actually find it hopeful. The world is a difficult place to exist with a lot of inequity and suffering. I've started to see my contributions to making a better planet as something to look forward to and not as a constant uphill struggle where I'm always wrong or not good enough. I'm learning to view my personal improvement and responsibilities as a positive part of my life, not as a chore. Yes, I need to work hard to do better but I'm teaching myself to want to do that hard work.

As much as I adored the writing process for what it helped me to understand about my own feelings, I'm also extremely interested in what the reader might get from the book. While I wait patiently for your feedback to flood through to me via postcards, let me tell you what I hope you get from it.

I hope the words on these pages don't make a final resting place in your brain. The messages in this book are only valuable if you take something from them and then let other people know about them. If you read something that you see as a truth, share it. Don't tell the publisher I said this, but re-gift this book to someone who you think it will speak to if they can't afford to buy it.

I know what it is like to have it suggested that you could be doing more all the time. It is draining and the first response can be one of resistance or annoyance. Who the heck is this fat gay guy telling me that I can be a better person? My advice for when the task of doing the right things feels overwhelming is to bite off smaller chunks. They are easier to digest. Put things into practice and soon they become every day. Doing better becomes part of your general approach to life.

If being inclusive within your veganism is a personal goal (and don't let me down this late in the game by saying it isn't), move through any challenges you encounter using small steps in order to solidify your good practice. If you feel overwhelmed, remind yourself that it is OK to feel that way as long as you take it on board as a learning experience. Looking deeply inside yourself in order to make changes to long held or ingrained ideas is understandably difficult. Actually, it can be brutally confronting.

One top tip I have for you? If you are challenged on your behaviour and you start to feel angry or resentful for being called out on it, it probably means you need to take a closer look at what exactly is being called out. It doesn't feel good to have it suggested that your behaviour might be contributing to the oppression of another person or entire communities. Our go to response is to get defensive and find a way to justify why we are participating in the offending language or behaviour.

You will learn to recognise this hot-headed reaction within yourself and begin to see it as a signpost that something needs to be explored. Honestly, you will start to appreciate feeling challenged and see it as an opportunity to do better.

Once you are aware that your behaviour surrounding a certain topic can be improved, talk to friends, re-read the parts of this book that spoke to you, watch videos online and do whatever you need to stay aware and well informed. People all over the planet are making and publishing positive and inclusive content in order to help you on your ethical vegan journey.

To put it simply, this book is my way of telling you that you are not alone. There are a lot of people you should be listening to when it comes to raising your awareness of social justice concerns. Some names have been mentioned previously in earlier chapters but many of them deserve repeating. Put a sticky note here and come back to these names. lauren Ornelas. Aph Ko. Christopher Sebastian

McJetters. Find them, read their words and consider what you can do better.

You are an important component of the future of ethical veganism and one of the people who should be heard. This book isn't to try to convince you that I am more qualified to speak on these topics or that I have the secret key to veganism. It has been written to encourage you to become the voice that your community needs. If my book has made you feel positive about the future of ethical veganism, get involved. Make yourself heard and work hard to elevate the voices of those often silenced or sidelined.

To the long-term vegans who have joined me for this journey, I need to offer up my awestruck admiration. I know what it is like to have lived through not very vegan-friendly days and those of you who have lived vegan lives longer than mine were really out in the wilderness. Your trailblazing ways and unwavering commitment to saving animals from unnecessary suffering have given people like me so much inspiration. Every direct action. Every small-town vegan fair. Every petition. Every awkward family situation through which you have suffered. Every bacon joke directed your way and deflected with style. Every carton of chalky plant-based milk you guzzled. Every animal you saved from a life of suffering. Thank you from the bottom of my chubby gay heart.

To the new vegans I would like to say welcome and extend my deep gratitude. Taking on veganism is one of the most life-altering decisions you can make and it isn't something undertaken lightly. Thank you for making the commitment to help improve outcomes for non-human animals. If it ever feels like a difficult responsibility to shoulder, remind yourself why you made the decision in the first place. Once you have a determined and solid reason for going vegan in your head and your heart, it gets easier every day. When you have that solid reason, you'll just know and you'll know there is no turning back. Welcome to the team!

To the not-yet-ready to commit to veganism (or future vegans if I'm going to be a glass half full kind of guy), I thank you for having an open mind and for taking the time to let my words into your world. I understand that we all really do want to do the right thing, or at least as many good things as possible, but I also understand that veganism can feel like the other side of a strange and confronting looking glass. Some good news? There are millions and millions of vegans living their lives right now as I close out this book and most of us are doing better than just getting by. People can survive and thrive whilst living a vegan lifestyle if they have access to animal alternatives and nutritious food.

When you are ready to explore a vegan life for yourself, I'm here to support you and so is every other vegan on the planet. You are not alone and you will not feel alone. Honestly, we don't ever shut up about it and we are right there when you need us. Every person who cares about protecting animals from suffering also cares about getting more people to go and stay vegan. When you are willing and able to expand your compassion, we've got your back. If funds are tight or other forces make committing to veganism difficult for you, tell those with more than you exactly what you need to feel supported. We are all in this together. Please understand that most vegans do not judge you harshly for not being vegan as the vast majority of us were once non-vegans ourselves. We don't think you are a bad person because we understand the powerful forces at play that work overtime to keep you eating, wearing and watching animals.

Writing this book has been a huge project for me but the message is immeasurably bigger. You and I can make decisions in our lives that will help to improve outcomes for animals. We can use our clout as consumers to shape the amount of suffering experienced on our planet. We can be unapologetically vegan and we can be kind and loving humans. We can be kind to other humans while we are at it. We can be proud of our choices to save animals from sad lives filled with pain and suffering.

Most importantly, we can do all of this together as part of a global community that looks out for everyone. We are infinitely more powerful together than we are as individuals. The strength in veganism comes from people being cherished, protected and celebrated.

Would you like to join me?

Resources

Vegan Basics

The Vegan Society vegansociety.com
Your one-stop destination for advice, guidance, nutrition insights and a slew of resources for new and existing vegans

Viva! viva.org.uk
Campaigns, recipes, resources and support. Especially helpful for transitioning to a vegan lifestyle

VeganEasy veganeasy.org
An easy to use consumer guide including advice on eating out, hidden food additives to watch out for, and useful shopping guides

Vegansaurus vegansaurus.com
Lifestyle blog with worldwide news, reviews, interviews and information useful for vegans both new and longterm

OUT AND ABOUT

HappyCow happycow.net
Extensive listings site featuring vegan and vegan-friendly restaurants and stores all over the planet. Available as a handy app

Barnivore barnivore.com
Web and app based searchable database to track vegan-suitable alcohol

TeenVGN teenvgn.com
The social network for young vegetarians and vegans (aged 12–19), and founders of the VGN Summer Camp

Todo Vegano todovegano.com todovegano.com/en/
Vegan restaurant and shopping database for Latin America. Includes English language version of the website

BEYOND VEGANISM

The Sistah Vegan Project sistahvegan.com
Unpacking food ethics, non-human animal compassion, anti-racism, black feminist theorising and critical food studies

Food Empowerment Project foodispower.org
Advice and guidelines on how to make ethical choices that
consider more than just non-human animals

Made in Hackney madeinhackney.org
London-based food equity group promoting accessible and
nutritious food for local communities. Website includes
resources and videos

ACKNOWLEDGEMENTS

This book was a labour of love and we all know how rocky that road can be. These people helped me stay the course, and they are owed my gratitude.

Thank you to Julio, Carlos, Iván and Richie for being in my life during the main writing sessions and for making me laugh (and sometimes cry).

Eternal gratitude to Kate Fox for thinking I was book-worthy and for being in my corner throughout the project. Liz Marvin deserves nothing short of a parade for her hard work in pulling the book together and dealing with me talking about the nuances of social justice concerns for vegans across several phone calls.

To everyone who contributed their voice to this book, I want to say thank you for your insights, kindness and time.

My final acknowledgement goes out to my partner, Josh. Behind the scenes of Fat Gay Vegan is another fat, gay vegan and I couldn't possibly overstate the importance of what Josh does to keep the show on the road. His contributions often go unrewarded. Thank you from the bottom of my heart.

ABOUT THE AUTHOR

Sean O'Callaghan is a vegan blogger who is known to his readers as Fat Gay Vegan. He splits his time between London and Mexico City. Sean is the founder and host of the Vegan Beer Fest UK event series, throwing parties for vegans in London, Sheffield, Glasgow, Manchester and beyond. He works as a freelance writer and has written for Vegan Life Magazine, The Los Angeles Times and Metro UK Online, and organises social events for vegans and their friends. Everyone's welcome.

NOURISH

EAT WELL, LIVE WELL